THE MIRROR EFFECT:
WHAT YOU SEE IS HOW YOU LEAD

10 COGNITIVE AND BEHAVIORAL PRACTICES TO BUILD AND SUSTAIN A HIGH-PERFORMING ORGANIZATIONAL CULTURE

Valentina Kordi

Contents

Dedication

To my beloved mother, who taught me the strength of resilience and the power of unconditional love.

Though Alzheimer's may steal moments, memories, and words, your grace, courage, and spirit remain indelible in my heart.

This book is for you, a testament to all you've given me, and a reminder that love transcends even the toughest of battles.

You are my inspiration, always.

About the Author

Valentina Kordi is a renowned Leadership and Executive Consultant, international keynote speaker, and best-selling author of the book "Success Is A Mind Game" with a robust background in mindset transformation and organizational culture. With 15 years of experience working with C-level executives and leaders across various industries all over the world, she has guided organizations in cultivating high-performing, engaged teams through emotional intelligence, resilience, and trust-based leadership strategies. Valentina holds a Bachelor's degree in Business Administration and a Master's degree in Human Resource Management and Organizational Psychology, and she has a Ph.D. Cand. in Organizational Psychology & Intervention, blending her academic expertise with real-world leadership consulting to drive impactful organizational change. She is passionate about helping leaders unlock their full potential, fostering positive work environments, and enhancing leadership effectiveness at all levels.

Her work is grounded in her commitment to empowering leaders to align their mindsets with successful, sustainable leadership practices that drive both individual and organizational success.

Introduction

In a world where businesses are continuously striving to outperform their competitors, the importance of a high-performing organizational culture cannot be overstated. Yet, many organizations struggle to create and sustain this type of culture. Why? The answer lies in leadership. A leader's mindset and behavior significantly influence the performance, development, and overall culture of the organization. This book, "The Mirror Effect: What You See Is How You Lead," delves into this concept, providing insights and practical strategies for leaders aiming to foster a productive and successful environment.

The mirror effect, as we will come to understand, is the reflection of a leader's mindset and behaviors on their team and the broader organization. This echo can be either positive or negative, constructive or destructive, depending on the leader's mindset. It's not just about what a leader does, but how they think, perceive, react, and interact. This book will guide you through 10 cognitive and behavioral practices that can help shape your mindset and, in turn, mirror a high-performing culture within your team and organization.

We'll explore the power of emotional intelligence and self-awareness, the role of visionary thinking, the importance of transparency and open communication, the value of inclusivity and diversity appreciation, the difference resilience and adaptability in a leader's attitude can make, and much more. Each chapter will provide actionable strategies and practices, backed by research and real-life examples, that you can implement immediately to start shaping your leadership mindset.

Whether you're a seasoned leader, a new manager, or an aspiring leader, this book will serve as a valuable guide. It will challenge your current perceptions, prompt introspection, and inspire change. As you turn each page, you'll gain a deeper understanding of the profound impact your mindset can have on your leadership style and, consequently, the performance and culture of your organization. As a leader, you are the mirror that your team looks into. What will they see? Let's begin the journey to find out.

Understanding the Mirror Effect

Leadership and its Reflection

It's a little after 9 o'clock at night. I've just finished my last session for the day. I take off my glasses, turn off my laptop, and think that it's finally about time to relax. It's been a long day of sessions since morning. Before I can finish my thought, my cell phone rings.

"Good evening, Valentina. It's D. Sorry for the hour; am I disturbing you?" I try to figure out who's on the other end of the line.

"D...?" I ask hesitantly.

"D., who used to work at X company! I contacted you by private message on LinkedIn after I purchased your book to ask for your help with a professional dilemma I was facing at the time. Without knowing me personally, you generously gave me your guidance and valuable time to help me out of that difficult situation. I am truly grateful to you for that. I told you then that you were the first person I would think of recommending if we needed a professional to train our staff or managers. That's why I called you!"

"Thank you so much, D., for your kind words. I did what I would have done anyway as a professional. But tell me, how can I help?"

"Since we've been in touch, I've made some changes in my professional life. I changed companies and industries. I now work for Company Z. You should know them. It is one of the largest Greek companies in its industry. A new challenge for me, as I left the previous one, which was a multinational, and now joined a family-owned and smaller company. I took up the position of Sales Director. However, I find that the company is suffering somewhat in terms of culture. They get very hung up on obstacles and constantly focus on why something can't be done. This phenomenon is very strong in my own sales team as well, and as you can see, it makes it difficult for me to do this work. So, I talked to the owners about you. I told them that you can be valuable in reshaping our culture. They want to see you. Can we set up a meeting?"

A few days later, I'm at the company's facility. I have a meeting with Mr. X, one of the owners and a board member, which is purely a "family affair." D. will also be at the meeting. I go up to the second floor. The secretary opens the door and directs me to the meeting room. As I walk, I glance around to see the faces and expressions of the employees, their posture, how they talk to each other, and how they answer the phones. It's something I always do when I visit a company. As I like to say when people ask me what a company culture is, "it's what you feel when you open the door and walk through the place. It's what you see on the faces of the employees." So, what I could see as I headed into the boardroom was a culture that was dour, miserable, and unwilling to do anything beyond the necessary and forced. "Let's have the meeting and see…" I thought.

I enter the meeting room and wait for a few minutes alone. The door opens, and I see D. He looks a little nervous. He sneaks a peek out the window and says to me, while simultaneously giving me his hand for a handshake:

"Valentina, welcome! I've been looking forward to seeing you! I hope that in our meeting today, you will be able to convince Mr. X that some things have to change here. I can't hide from you that I'm beginning to worry whether I made the right choice in coming here."

The door opens. In walks a tall, stocky man with gray hair.

"Good evening, Ms. Kordi. I am Mr. X, one of the owners of our company. D. spoke about you enthusiastically, and I thought we should invite you to see how and if you can help us…"

After giving me a lengthy description of the company's journey and their products, he then gets into the subject.

"Our problem here, Ms. Kordi, is that the employees are with a 'no' ready in their mouths. Especially with the sales team, which is supposed to be our most combative team. The team is made up of both salespeople, who have been with us for many years and some new ones. The common thread that almost all of them have in common is that they see obstacles everywhere and want to do what is only easy and what they have been doing for so long. For example, they have recently added some new ones to our product range. Our salespeople continue to sell, however, only the ones they have been selling so far. They turn back from visiting customers, and everyone says, "But it's hard to shift them to the new products. They're not interested; they want to keep buying the old codes."

I tell them to come up with ideas on how to turn customers to start ordering the new codes and they keep telling me about why that can't be done! It's getting very frustrating. The company made an investment and is losing money like this. Their constant argument is that there was no reason to put in new products. They were working fine with the codes they already had for years. But I don't hear any solutions! Only problems, obstacles, and objections. They go out to see customers, and several times, instead of coming back with orders, they come back with problems and empty hands.

You know, I am a person who always focuses on solutions. I'm flexible and don't have a hard time making changes. I want our staff to do the same! I want them to become receptive to change. I want them to come back and have orders in their hands. I want them to be able to convince customers to try the new products and not come back to tell me that maybe it's better to keep selling the old ones. Can you do a seminar and get them to change their minds?"

"Look," I reply. "I don't do brain surgery. I'm not a neurosurgeon. My expertise is indeed in changing people's mindsets at work. However, this is a whole process. You don't change their whole mindset in one seminar. You need to create a plan and a program to develop your salespeople and change their mindset. This requires several steps and stages.."

"Listen to me, Ms. Kordi!" he cuts me off abruptly. "We don't have time to waste. We can't invest too much time and money to change mindsets. That's impossible, I would say! I can't keep them busy for hours on anything but sales and seeing customers. I would say we should do a 4-5 hour seminar, so they can hear what I want them to understand and apply it, just like we do with other trainings. There's no chance to do anything else. I can't have them sitting around for longer instead of bringing me sales!"

"Have the 4-5 hour training sessions you've done so far gotten you results?" I asked him.

"No, but I don't think we can do anything else. Just this!"

Culture is "mirrored" at the head of a company. And the story above is a prime example of this mirroring, as it occurs in all businesses, differently, of course, in each one. So, the owner was resentful of the negative and restrictive mindset carried by the employees of his business. He was asking them to 'step outside the box,' to be flexible and focus on solutions, not obstacles. To embrace the new and not get stuck in a habit. Yet he was the first to do just the opposite! In our conversation, he gave me all the reasons why nothing but a 4-5 hour training could be done, even though it was something they had already tried and it wasn't effective. He brought forward all the "can'ts" and "no's." He didn't even have the patience to tell him what kind of program I had in mind. He was quick to dismiss it out of hand and focus on what couldn't be done. He wanted to turn back to a path he had already walked and felt safe, regardless of whether it wasn't effective.'

The Mirror Effect tells us that our mindset as leaders, is reflected back to us in the results we see within our teams and organizations. Like a mirror reflecting our image, our attitude, beliefs, and actions as leaders are mirrored in the performance and behavior of our team. This subchapter aims to delve deeper into the concept of leadership and its reflection, exploring how our mindset as leaders impacts our team and the overall performance of the organization.

Consider for a moment the concept of a mirror. A mirror doesn't judge, it doesn't alter, it simply reflects. It provides a clear and accurate reflection of what stands before it. Similarly, our leadership style and mindset are reflected back to us through the performance and attitude of our team. If we wish to see a positive change in our team, we must first look at improving and modifying our own mindset and behavior.

A leader with a positive and solutions-oriented mindset will likely foster a team that is motivated, enthusiastic, and eager to learn and grow. On the other hand, a leader with a negative or problems and obstacles-oriented mindset might see their team struggle with motivation, innovation, and growth. This is the Mirror Effect in action.

The power of this Mirror Effect lies in its simplicity. It puts the onus of change and improvement firmly in our hands as leaders. We are not powerless observers in our organizations. Instead, we have the power and responsibility to influence our team's performance and attitude through our own mindset and behavior.

So, how can we use this Mirror Effect to our advantage? By understanding that our leadership style is a reflection of our mindset, we can start to consciously cultivate a positive and growth-oriented mindset. This involves challenging our limiting beliefs, embracing and failure as a learning opportunity, and continuously seeking growth and improvement through change and development.

Moreover, effective communication is a crucial aspect of a positive leadership mindset. An open, transparent, and empathetic communication style can help in building trust, fostering collaboration, and encouraging innovation within the team. Remember, as a leader, your communication style is also reflected back to you in the form of your team's communication patterns.

Additionally, emotional intelligence is another key aspect of a positive leadership mindset. By understanding and managing our emotions, we can better navigate the complexities and challenges of leadership. This emotional intelligence is mirrored back to us in the emotional health and resilience of our team.

The Mirror Effect is a powerful tool for self-improvement and leadership development. It provides us with a clear, unfiltered view of our leadership impact. By understanding and leveraging this effect, we can become more effective and influential leaders.

Remember, leadership is not about wielding power but about empowering others. And this empowerment starts with our own mindset. As we begin to reflect positivity, growth, effective communication, and emotional intelligence in our leadership, we will start to see these qualities mirrored back to us in our team and organization.

So, let's take a moment to look in the mirror. What does your leadership reflection tell you? And more importantly, what are you going to do about it? The power to change and improve is in your hands. Use the Mirror Effect to your advantage and become the leader you aspire to be.

Influence on Company Culture

Leadership mindset is a powerful tool, a catalyst, capable of transforming not only the individual but also the environment they inhabit. One of the most profound areas where this transformation becomes evident is within the company culture.

The essence of company culture is the shared ethos and values that drive the organization. It's the collective heartbeat of a company, influencing every aspect of its operations, from decision-making processes to employee engagement and customer satisfaction. The leader, with their mindset, acts as the pacemaker for this heartbeat.

A leader's mindset is like a mirror. It reflects their beliefs, attitudes, and behaviors, which, in turn, are absorbed and mirrored by the team. If a leader embodies a growth mindset, their employees are more likely to adopt the same. They'll view challenges as opportunities for learning and improvement rather than roadblocks. They'll be more open to innovative ideas and unorthodox solutions. This openness fosters a culture of creativity and innovation where employees feel valued and motivated to contribute their best.

On the other hand, a leader with a fixed mindset can stifle growth and innovation. Such leaders often view failure as a reflection of personal inadequacy, and this fear of failure trickles down to the team. As a result, employees may become risk-averse, settling for safe and conventional solutions. This can lead to a stagnant company culture, where innovation and progress are stifled.

A leader's mindset also influences the interpersonal dynamics within a company. Leaders who operate from a mindset of trust, respect, and empathy foster a culture where these values are held in high regard. Such a culture promotes healthy communication and collaboration, leading to a more cohesive and effective team.

In contrast, leaders with a competitive or ego-driven mindset may create a culture of rivalry and mistrust. In such an environment, employees may feel compelled to outdo each other, leading to stress, burnout, and a toxic work environment. The company may achieve short-term gains, but in the long run, such a culture erodes employee morale and productivity.

Moreover, a leader's mindset influences their approach to employee development. Leaders with a growth mindset see potential in each employee and invest time and resources in nurturing their skills and talents. They recognize that their success is intrinsically linked to the success of their team. This approach cultivates a culture of continuous learning and development, where employees are encouraged to grow and evolve.

In contrast, leaders with a fixed mindset may view employee development as a needless expense, focusing solely on immediate results. Such a perspective can lead to high employee turnover and a culture of short-termism.

In essence, the leader's mindset is the invisible hand that shapes the company culture. It's the lens through which they view the world, and it shapes their actions and decisions, which ultimately mold the company culture. Therefore, cultivating a positive and growth-oriented mindset is not just a personal journey but a strategic move toward building a thriving, innovative, and resilient company culture.

In the mirror of leadership, every thought, every belief, and every action is reflected. By consciously choosing a mindset of growth, trust, and empathy, leaders can significantly influence the company culture, creating an environment where both the company and its employees can flourish. This is the power of the mirror effect. This is the power of the leadership mindset.

Practice Nr. 1: Perception
& Emotional Intelligence

Leadership is more than just guiding a team toward achieving goals; it's about understanding the deeper dynamics at play, both within yourself and in those you lead. The mirror effect suggests that what you see in yourself—your motivations, strengths, weaknesses, insecurities, fears, and even your emotional triggers—is what you project onto your team. This projection influences how they perceive you, how they perform, and ultimately, the culture of your workplace.

In this chapter, we explore the powerful combination of perception, emotional intelligence, and self-awareness in leadership. We'll delve into how these elements shape not only your relationships with your team but also the very foundation of your organizational culture.

I once worked with a leader of a fast-growing marketing agency. He was brilliant, driven, and incredibly focused on achieving results. His company was on the brink of securing a major deal, and he was determined to push his team to meet the demanding deadlines. However, in his relentless pursuit of success, he often overlooked the emotional well-being of her employees.

His leadership style was influenced by his own fears and insecurities. He had always believed that success was tied to relentless hard work and high expectations—values instilled in him from a young age. He feared that if he didn't push his team hard enough, they would fall short, and the company would fail. These fears drove him to micromanage, criticize, and dismiss his team's concerns, thinking that this was the best way to achieve results.

One day, during a critical meeting, one of his top developers hesitantly raised a concern. "The team is really struggling with the workload. We've been working late nights for weeks, and people are burning out. I think we need to consider adjusting the timeline."

The leader, triggered by his fear of failure, immediately dismissed his concerns. "We can't afford to slow down now. This deal is crucial, and everyone needs to push through. We've all worked hard to get here, and it's just a little longer," he said, her tone leaving no room for further discussion.

The developer, visibly deflated, nodded and stayed quiet for the rest of the meeting. The atmosphere in the room was tense—others on the team looked equally exhausted but didn't dare speak up. Over the next few weeks, productivity began to decline. The developer himself, who had been one of the most committed employees, started missing deadlines, and his usually high-quality work began to slip. The tension in the office grew, and the once cohesive team started to fragment.

Realizing that something was wrong, the leader reached out to me for help. During our first session, I asked him, "What do you think is driving your need to push the team so hard?"

He hesitated before replying, "I guess I've always believed that success comes from hard work and pushing through obstacles. I'm afraid that if I don't keep the pressure on, we'll fall behind."

"That fear is understandable," I acknowledged. "But how do you think it's affecting your team?"

The leader looked troubled. "I know they're stressed, but I'm just trying to make sure we succeed."

"Let's take a step back," I suggested. "What if your fear of failure is actually holding you and your team back? When you lead from a place of fear, it's easy to overlook the emotional and psychological needs of your team. What if, instead of pushing harder, you started leading with empathy and emotional intelligence? How might things change if you were more aware of how your actions were impacting your team's morale and performance?"

He was silent for a moment, reflecting. "I've never really thought about it that way. I guess I've been so focused on the end goal that I've lost sight of how we're getting there."

"Exactly," I said. "Leadership isn't just about achieving results—it's about how you achieve them. Your self-awareness, or lack thereof, directly influences your leadership style and the culture you're creating. By becoming more aware of your own triggers and motivations, you can lead with greater empathy and emotional intelligence, ultimately fostering a more positive and productive work environment."

Determined to make a change, the leader began to work on his self-awareness. He started by reflecting on his own fears and insecurities and how they were influencing his leadership style. He also began to practice empathy, making a conscious effort to listen to his team's concerns and validate their experiences.

The next day, he gathered her team for a meeting. This time, instead of diving straight into work, he opened up the floor for discussion. "I realize that I've been pushing you all really hard lately, and I want to apologize for not being more considerate of how this is affecting you. I'd like to hear how you're feeling and discuss how we can support each other to get through this."

The team was initially surprised by his shift in tone, but slowly, they began to share their frustrations and concerns. He listened attentively, acknowledging their challenges and expressing his gratitude for their hard work. Together, they brainstormed ways to adjust the workload and timeline without compromising the deal.

This small act of empathy, combined with his growing self-awareness, made a significant difference. The team felt heard and valued, and their energy began to return. The developer, in particular, was reinvigorated and started producing his best work again. In the end, not only did they meet the deadline, but they also secured the deal—proving that leading with empathy, emotional intelligence, and self-awareness is key to sustainable success.

The Power of Perception

The way we perceive ourselves and the world around us has a significant impact on our ability to lead. Our perception, essentially, is the lens through which we view our reality. It is our personal interpretation of the world, shaped by our experiences, beliefs, values, and assumptions. This lens can either limit or expand our potential, affect our relationships, and ultimately impact our leadership effectiveness.

Imagine you're at the helm of a ship. The ship represents your department or your organization. Your perception is the compass that guides you. If your compass is accurate, you will navigate successfully. However, if it's skewed, you might find yourself off course, even lost. Therefore, understanding and managing your perception is crucial for effective leadership.

Perception influences our decision-making process. As leaders, every decision we make is based on our understanding and interpretation of the information available to us. If our perception is skewed, our decisions may not yield the desired results. For instance, if we perceive a challenge as a threat, we might respond defensively, leading to conflict or missed opportunities. On the other hand, if we see the same challenge as an opportunity, we might respond proactively, leading to innovation and growth.

Our perception also affects our communication. The way we perceive others influences how we interact with them. If we perceive someone as untrustworthy, our interactions with them will likely be guarded and cautious. Conversely, if we perceive them as reliable, our interactions will likely be open and collaborative. As leaders, our perception can either build bridges or walls in our relationships. It can either foster trust and collaboration or breed distrust and conflict.

Moreover, our perception shapes our self-image and self-esteem. How we perceive ourselves determines our confidence in our abilities and our worthiness of success. If we perceive ourselves as inadequate or unworthy, we might shy away from taking risks or pursuing opportunities, limiting our growth and potential. On the contrary, if we perceive ourselves as capable and deserving, we might take bold actions and seize opportunities, propelling our growth and success.

As leaders, we must be aware of the power of our perception. We must continually question and challenge our assumptions and beliefs to ensure they are accurate and beneficial. We must be open to new experiences and perspectives to broaden our understanding and enrich our worldview. We must also foster a positive self-perception to build our confidence and resilience.

It's important to note that managing our perception does not mean ignoring or denying reality. It means understanding that our perception is just one interpretation of reality and being open to other interpretations. It means recognizing that our perception is malleable and can be changed.

Leadership is a journey of self-discovery and growth. The first step on this journey is understanding the power of perception. The next step is harnessing this power to navigate successfully, make wise decisions, communicate effectively, and boost our self-esteem. By mastering our perception, we can become more effective leaders and create a positive impact in our lives and the lives of those we lead but have a huge impact on the workplace culture that will be molded through this perception.

Remember, perception is not just about what you see; it's about how you see. So, how do you see yourself? How do you see the world around you? How do you see your role as a leader? The answers to these questions will shape your leadership culture and, ultimately, your team's perception and your organization's culture.

Emotional Intelligence and Its Impact on Leadership

Emotional Intelligence (EQ) is the ability to recognize, understand, manage, and influence your own emotions and the emotions of others (Salovey & Mayer, 1990). As a leader, your emotional intelligence directly affects your ability to communicate, manage stress, make decisions, and navigate social complexities within your organization.

Daniel Goleman (1995), a pioneer in the study of emotional intelligence, identifies five key components of EI:

1. **Self-Awareness**: The ability to recognize and understand your own emotions and how they affect your thoughts and behavior.

2. **Self-Regulation**: The ability to control impulsive feelings and behaviors, manage your emotions in healthy ways, take initiative, and adapt to changing circumstances.

3. **Motivation**: A passion to work for reasons beyond money or status, driven by an inner vision of what is important in life and the joy that comes from accomplishing meaningful goals.

4. **Empathy**: The ability to understand the emotions of others, to treat people according to their emotional reactions, and to build strong, authentic relationships.

5. **Social Skills**: Proficiency in managing relationships and building networks, finding common ground, and building rapport.

In leadership, these components are crucial. When you are emotionally intelligent, you are better equipped to lead with empathy, which is the cornerstone of creating a culture where employees feel valued, understood, and motivated.

The Mindset of an Emotionally Intelligent Leader

To lead with emotional intelligence, you must first cultivate the right mindset. This mindset is rooted in the belief that emotions matter in the workplace and that understanding and managing these emotions is key to unlocking the potential of your team.

1. Prioritizing People Over Tasks

An emotionally intelligent leader understands that the people they lead are not just resources to accomplish tasks; they are individuals with unique experiences, emotions, and motivations. By prioritizing people over tasks, you create an environment where employees feel respected and valued, leading to higher engagement and productivity. Now, don't get me wrong! That doesn't mean neglecting goals, commitments or timelines. It means that you need to always remember that all these are done by humans, so don't neglect or belittle the importance of even though your team members are there to work, they are still human beings and their emotions might make or break the outcome you're after.

2. Embracing Vulnerability

Many leaders believe that showing vulnerability is a sign of weakness. However, embracing vulnerability is actually a sign of strength. When you are open about your own challenges and emotions, you create a safe space for your team to do the same. This openness fosters trust, which is essential for a high-performing culture.

3. Viewing Challenges as Opportunities for Growth

An emotionally intelligent leader sees challenges as opportunities to grow, both personally and as a team. When you approach obstacles with a mindset of growth rather than fear or frustration, you encourage your team to do the same, cultivating resilience and innovation.

4. Valuing Continuous Learning

Emotional intelligence is not a static trait; it's something that can be developed and improved over time. A leader with an EI-focused mindset is committed to continuous learning—seeking feedback, reflecting on experiences, and making adjustments to improve their emotional intelligence.

Behavioral Practices of an Emotionally Intelligent Leader

Once you have cultivated the right mindset, the next step is to translate it into specific behaviors that reinforce a culture of empathy and emotional intelligence. These behaviors serve as the mirror through which your team sees the values you wish to instill within the organization.

1. Active Listening

Active listening is the cornerstone of EQ. It's more than just hearing what someone is saying; it's about fully engaging with the speaker, understanding their message, and responding thoughtfully.

Behavioral Practices:

- **Maintain eye contact:** This shows that you are fully present in the conversation.

- **Avoid interrupting:** Let the speaker finish their thoughts before responding.

- **Paraphrase and summarize:** Reflect back on what you've heard to ensure understanding.

- **Ask open-ended questions:** Encourage the speaker to share more about their thoughts and feelings by starting your questions with how, what, or why.

By practicing active listening, you show your team that you value their input and are genuinely interested in their well-being, which fosters a culture of mutual respect and trust.

2. Regular Self-Reflection and Emotional Regulation:

Regular self-reflection and Emotional regulation are about becoming aware and managing your thoughts and emotions, particularly in stressful situations. Leaders who can maintain their composure and respond thoughtfully rather than react impulsively are better able to navigate challenges and make sound decisions.

Behavioral Practices:

- **Pause before responding:** When faced with a stressful situation, take a moment to collect your thoughts before reacting.

- **Practice mindfulness:** Regular mindfulness exercises can help you stay grounded and focused, even in high-pressure situations.

- **Reflect on Personal Motives, Biases and Triggers:** Understand what drives you personally to do what you do, your biases and emotional triggers. Recognize how these factors influence your behavior, attitude and decision-making as a leader.

- **Acknowledge your emotions:** Recognize your feelings without being overwhelmed by them. This allows you to choose a measured response.

By demonstrating emotional regulation, you set an example for your team, showing them that challenges can be met with calm and thoughtful action rather than panic or impulsivity.

3. Showing Genuine Appreciation: Building a Positive Culture

Recognition and appreciation are powerful tools for building a positive workplace culture. When leaders show genuine appreciation for their team's efforts, it boosts morale, increases motivation, and fosters a sense of belonging.

Behavioral Practices:

- **Give specific praise:** Instead of generic compliments, acknowledge specific actions or behaviors that you appreciate in your team members.

- **Celebrate successes:** Take time to celebrate both small and large achievements, whether through formal recognition programs or informal gestures.

- **Express gratitude regularly:** Make it a habit to thank your team members for their hard work and contributions.

By regularly showing appreciation, you reinforce a culture of positivity and recognition where employees feel valued and motivated to perform at their best.

4. Practicing Empathy in Decision-Making

Empathy should be a guiding principle in your decision-making process. When leaders consider the impact of their decisions on others, they build trust and loyalty within their teams.

Behavioral Practices:

- **Put yourself in others' shoes:** Before making a decision, consider how it will affect different members of your team.

- **Seek input from those affected:** Involve your team in the decision-making process, especially when the outcome will have a significant impact on them.

- **Communicate the reasoning behind decisions:** When you explain the "why" behind your decisions, it helps your team understand your perspective and reduces resistance.

By leading with empathy in decision-making, you create a culture of inclusivity and fairness where employees feel that their voices are heard and respected.

5. Encouraging Open and Honest Communication

Open communication is the lifeblood of a healthy organizational culture. Leaders who encourage transparency and honesty create an environment where issues can be addressed before they escalate and where innovative ideas can flourish.

Behavioral Practices:

- **Foster an open-door policy:** Make it clear that employees can come to you with concerns, ideas, or feedback at any time.

- **Encourage feedback:** Actively seek out feedback from your team and be open to constructive criticism.

Science-Based Insight

Neuroscience research shows that leaders with high emotional intelligence (EQ) significantly impact their employees' brain function, particularly in areas related to social behavior and emotional regulation. Mirror neurons—neurons that fire both when an individual performs an action and when they observe someone else performing the same action—are a critical factor in this. These neurons are essential for empathy and social bonding, meaning that when a leader exhibits emotional intelligence and empathy, the mirror neurons in their employees' brains are activated. This leads to stronger social connections, lower stress levels, and an increased sense of trust and safety in the workplace, fostering higher engagement and collaboration (Henley, 2019).

Moreover, emotionally intelligent leadership has been shown to increase the release of oxytocin, a hormone associated with trust and social bonding, further reinforcing a high-performing and positive workplace culture (Orloff, 2022).

Putting pen to paper

Exercise: Enhancing Self-Awareness for Better Leadership

To help you develop greater self-awareness and lead with empathy and emotional intelligence, take the following steps:

Step 1: Reflect on Your Leadership Style

- Set aside 15 minutes in a quiet space. Reflect on some recent leadership experiences. Ask yourself:

  - What emotions did I experience during these challenging moments?

  - How did I react to those emotions?

  - What motivated my decisions and actions?

  - Did I consider the emotional and psychological needs of my team?

    - How did my behavior impact the morale and performance of my team?

Step 2: Identify Your Triggers

- List the situations or behaviors that trigger strong emotional reactions in you (e.g., frustration, anger, anxiety). Consider how these triggers influence your leadership decisions and interactions with your team.

Step 3: Evaluate Your Strengths and Weaknesses

- Identify your key strengths as a leader and how you can leverage them to enhance your team's performance.

- Acknowledge your weaknesses and consider how they might be affecting your leadership. Develop an action plan to address these areas, whether through personal development, delegation, or seeking feedback from others.

Step 4: Practice Empathy

- Commit to actively listening to your team members. During your next interaction, focus entirely on what they are saying without interrupting, judging or planning your response. Reflect back on what you've heard to show understanding and ask open-ended questions to explore their perspective further. Evaluate afterward, on a scale of 1-10 (not satisfied at all – totally happy with), how well you did with practicing empathy during that interaction. Notice also what did you do well and where you need further improvement.

Step 5: Seek Feedback

- Ask your team for feedback on your leadership style. Encourage them to be honest about how your behavior impacts their work and morale. Use this feedback to adjust your approach and improve your leadership effectiveness.

- To make it even easier, ask them 4 simple questions: What they like about your leadership style and what you should keep? What they would like to see you change? What they would like to see you doing more of, and what they would like to see you doing less of?

Step 6: Set Personal Goals

- Set specific, measurable goals for improving your self-awareness, empathy, and emotional intelligence. Track your progress and adjust your goals as needed to continue growing as a leader.

By completing this exercise, you'll gain a deeper understanding of your leadership style and its impact on your team. This self-awareness will enable you to lead with greater empathy and emotional intelligence, creating a high-performing, positive workplace culture.

Exercise: The Empathy Mapping Session

Objective: To enhance your ability to understand and empathize with your team members by mapping out their emotional experiences in different work situations.

Instructions:

1. **Choose a recent team interaction:** Reflect on a recent team meeting, one-on-one conversation, or project discussion where emotions were high, whether due to stress, excitement, or conflict.

2. **Create an empathy map:** On a sheet of paper or a digital document, divide the page into four quadrants labeled as follows:

   - **What they said:** Write down the words and phrases your team member(s) used during the interaction.

   - **What they did:** Note their body language, facial expressions, and actions during the interaction.

- **What they were thinking:** Based on their words and actions, infer what thoughts might have been going through their mind.

- **What they were feeling:** Identify the emotions they might have been experiencing, such as frustration, excitement, anxiety, or relief.

3. **Analyze the map:** Reflect on the empathy map you've created. Consider how your team member(s) might have felt during the interaction and how your response could have either alleviated or exacerbated those emotions.

4. **Plan an empathetic response:** Based on your analysis, think about how you could approach similar situations in the future with greater empathy. Consider how you could adjust your communication, behavior, or decision-making to better support your team's emotional needs.

5. **Implement and reflect:** In your next team interaction, consciously apply the empathetic approaches you've planned. Afterward, reflect on how your behavior influenced the outcome and how your team responded emotionally.

Avoiding Leadership Pitfalls:
The Dark Side of Emotional Detachment

While empathy and emotional intelligence are essential for effective leadership, it's important to recognize the pitfalls of their absence. Leaders who are emotionally detached or lack empathy can create a toxic work environment, leading to disengagement, low morale, and high turnover.

1. Emotional Detachment and Disengagement

Leaders who fail to connect with their team on an emotional level may appear distant or uninterested. This emotional detachment can lead to disengagement, as employees feel undervalued and unsupported.

Consequences:

- **Low morale:** A lack of empathy from leadership can result in low employee morale, reducing productivity and job satisfaction.

- **Increased turnover:** Disengaged employees are more likely to leave the organization, leading to higher turnover and associated costs.

- **Missed opportunities:** Emotionally detached leaders may miss important cues from their team, such as early signs of burnout or dissatisfaction, resulting in unresolved issues that could have been addressed.

2. Ineffective Communication and Misunderstandings

Leaders who lack emotional intelligence may struggle with communication, leading to misunderstandings and confusion. Without empathy, they may fail to grasp the nuances of their team's concerns or misinterpret feedback.

Consequences:

- **Confusion and frustration:** Poor communication can lead to confusion and frustration among team members, hindering their ability to perform effectively.

- **Decreased collaboration:** Misunderstandings and miscommunication can erode trust and collaboration, making it difficult for teams to work together effectively.

- **Loss of trust:** When leaders are perceived as out of touch with their team's emotions, they risk losing the trust and respect of their employees.

3. Ignoring the Human Element in Decision-Making

Leaders who prioritize tasks and metrics over the human element may make decisions that negatively impact their team's well-being. Without empathy, they may overlook the emotional and psychological effects of their decisions, leading to a demotivated and disengaged workforce.

Consequences:

- **Employee dissatisfaction:** Decisions made without considering the human impact can lead to employee dissatisfaction and resentment.

- **Reduced loyalty:** Employees who feel that their well-being is not a priority are less likely to be loyal to the organization.

- **Negative workplace culture:** A culture that prioritizes tasks over people can become toxic, with high levels of stress, burnout, and disengagement.

Conclusion: Leading with Self-Awareness and Emotional Intelligence as the First Step to Success

Self-awareness and emotional intelligence are not just soft skills—they are powerful leadership tools that can transform an organization.

By cultivating these qualities in yourself, you set the tone for a workplace culture that is positive, high-performing, and resilient.

In this chapter, we've explored how the mindset of an emotionally intelligent leader translates into specific behaviors that foster a culture of empathy, trust, and collaboration. We've also examined the ripple effects of these behaviors on organizational culture and the pitfalls of their absence.

As you continue to develop your leadership skills, remember that what you see in your team is a reflection of what you cultivate in yourself. By leading with empathy and emotional intelligence, you not only create a better work environment for your team but also set the stage for sustainable success.

In the following chapters, we will build on this foundation, exploring additional cognitive and behavioral practices that will help you refine your leadership approach and create a thriving, high-performing organizational culture. Together, we will uncover the full spectrum of leadership qualities that will empower you to lead with confidence, compassion, and clarity.

Practice Nr. 2: Visionary Thinking

Visionary thinking is the cornerstone of effective leadership. It is the ability to look beyond the present, foresee what could be, and then guide your organization toward that future with clarity and purpose. Visionary leaders are not only dreamers but also doers—they are able to translate their vision into actionable strategies that inspire and mobilize their teams.

In this chapter of The Mirror Effect: What You See, Is How You Lead!, we will explore how visionary thinking shapes organizational culture and drives success. We will examine the mindset necessary to cultivate visionary thinking and the behaviors that bring it to life, ultimately creating a workplace where people are inspired, aligned, and committed to a common goal.

I once worked with a leader named T., the COO of a mid-sized manufacturing company. T. was exceptional at optimizing processes and meeting quarterly targets, but he struggled with visionary thinking. His focus remained firmly on the present— how to improve efficiency and cut costs. However, the company's growth had begun to plateau, and competitors were gaining ground with innovative products. The board was eager for new strategies to reignite the company's market position.

During a strategic planning meeting, L., the Head of Marketing, suggested exploring new markets and investing in cutting-edge technology that could set them apart. She painted a picture of where the industry was heading and how their company could lead the charge. T., however, quickly dismissed her ideas. "We need to stick to what we know best," he said, concerned about the risks and costs. His reluctance to consider new possibilities left the team feeling stifled and uninspired.

As the months passed, the company's stagnation became more apparent. Competitors began launching innovative products, and their market share started slipping. The board grew increasingly concerned, and T. felt the pressure mounting. Realizing he needed to shift his approach, T. reached out to me for guidance.

During one of our sessions, I decided to challenge T.'s perspective. "T., you've built a strong company by focusing on what works today. But let me ask you this: where do you see your company in five years? What's the legacy you want to leave behind?"

T. hesitated. "I want the company to remain strong, to keep growing, but... I'm not sure how to achieve that. We're doing everything right, but it feels like we're stuck."

"That's because you're so focused on the present that you're missing the opportunities of the future," I explained. "Visionary potential beyond what's immediately in front of you. Imagine if you allowed yourself to think beyond the current constraints. What could your company become?"

T. looked thoughtful. "But what if these new ideas fail? What if the risks outweigh the benefits?"

"Failure is always a possibility," I acknowledged, "but so is success. And often, the greatest successes come from taking calculated risks, from daring to envision something greater than what exists today. The companies that lead their industries are the ones willing to innovate to step into the unknown with confidence. Your team is ready to think big—they just need your support to do so."

T. sat quietly for a moment, then sighed. "I've been so focused on maintaining what we have that I've forgotten to consider where we could go."

"Exactly," I said. "Your role as a leader isn't just to manage the present; it's to inspire your team with a vision of the future. They're waiting for you to lead them there."

This conversation marked a turning point for T. He began to see the value in visionary thinking and understood that his role was not just to protect the company's current success but to guide it toward future opportunities.

Determined to change, T. re-engaged his leadership team with a new perspective. In the next strategic meeting, he revisited L.'s proposal with genuine interest. "Let's explore these new markets and technologies," he said, surprising his team. "I want us to think big, to imagine where we can take this company in the next five years."

The shift in T.'s approach breathed new life into the company. The team felt energized, knowing they were working towards an exciting and ambitious future. Over time, the company regained its competitive edge, launching innovative products that captured the market's attention.

T. learned that visionary thinking wasn't just about dreaming—it was about leading with a sense of purpose and inspiring others to believe in a brighter future. And it all began with a conversation that challenged him to look beyond the present and embrace the possibilities of tomorrow.

Understanding Visionary Thinking
and Its Role in Leadership

Visionary thinking is more than just having a long-term goal or a plan. It's about seeing the bigger picture, understanding the trends that will shape the future, and recognizing the opportunities and challenges that lie ahead. Leaders with visionary thinking possess the foresight to anticipate change and the wisdom to navigate their organization through it.

Visionary leaders act as the architects of their organization's future. They create a compelling vision that not only sets the direction but also inspires others to follow. This vision becomes a critical element of the organizational culture, influencing everything from strategic decisions to everyday interactions. It provides a sense of purpose and direction that unites and motivates the entire team.

The Mindset of a Visionary Leader

To lead with visionary thinking, you must first adopt a mindset that is expansive, forward-looking, and deeply aligned with your organization's core values. This mindset allows you to see beyond the immediate challenges and to imagine what is possible, even when the path forward is not yet clear.

1. Seeing Beyond the Present

A visionary leader is always thinking ahead, considering how today's actions will shape tomorrow's outcomes. They are not confined by the present limitations and are constantly scanning the horizon for new opportunities and potential risks.

Mindset: Embrace the idea that the future is not a distant reality but something you create through the decisions you make today. Understand that while the present is important, it is merely a stepping stone toward a greater future.

2. Believing in the Power of Purpose

Visionary leaders understand that people are driven by a sense of purpose. They believe that a compelling vision provides meaning and motivation, inspiring people to contribute their best efforts, even in the face of challenges.

Mindset: Cultivate a deep belief in the power of purpose. Recognize that when your team understands the "why" behind their work, they are more engaged, committed, and aligned with the organization's goals.

3. Embracing Innovation and Change

Visionary leaders are not afraid of change; they welcome it as an opportunity for growth and innovation. They understand that the world is constantly evolving and that to stay ahead, their organization must be willing to adapt and innovate.

Mindset: View innovation as a critical component of progress. Understand that achieving a vision requires a willingness to explore new ideas and adapt to changing circumstances.

4. Commitment to Long-Term Thinking

Visionary leaders are not focused on short-term gains at the expense of long-term success. They understand that building a sustainable organization requires patience, perseverance, and a commitment to the future.

Mindset: Prioritize long-term success over short-term wins. Recognize that true leadership involves making decisions that will benefit the organization in the years to come, even if they require sacrifices in the present.

Behavioral Practices for Leading with Visionary Thinking

Once you have cultivated a visionary mindset, the next step is to translate that mindset into specific behaviors that inspire and guide your team. These behaviors are crucial for embedding the vision into the organizational culture, ensuring that it becomes a living, breathing part of the organization's identity.

1. Articulating a Clear and Compelling Vision

A vision is only as powerful as your ability to communicate it. Visionary leaders excel at articulating their vision in a way that is clear, inspiring, and relatable. They use their vision to guide strategic decisions, rally their team, and keep everyone aligned with the organization's goals.

Behavioral Practices:

- **Craft a compelling narrative:** Frame your vision as a story that captures the imagination of your team. Use vivid language and examples to illustrate what the future could look like.

- **Be clear and concise:** Avoid jargon and overly complex or vague language. Your vision should be easy to understand by everyone in the organization.

- **Tie the vision to values:** Connect your vision to the core values of the organization. This helps employees see the vision as an extension of what the organization stands for.

By clearly articulating your vision, you provide a sense of direction and purpose that motivates your team and aligns their efforts with the future you want to create.

2. Aligning Actions with the Vision

Visionary leaders ensure that their actions—and the actions of their team—are consistently aligned with the vision. They understand that every decision, no matter how small, should move the organization closer to its desired future.

Behavioral Practices:

- **Set strategic priorities:** Identify the key initiatives that will drive progress toward the vision. Focus your team's efforts on these priorities and avoid distractions.

- **Lead by example:** Demonstrate your commitment to the vision through your own actions. When your team sees you making decisions that align with the vision, they are more likely to do the same.

- **Hold others accountable:** Ensure that your team understands the importance of aligning their actions with the vision. Hold them accountable for making decisions and taking actions that support the organization's long-term goals.

By consistently aligning actions with the vision, you create a culture of purpose and direction where every decision contributes to the larger goals of the organization.

3. Inspiring and Engaging Your Team

A vision is most powerful when it is shared and embraced by the entire organization. Visionary leaders excel at inspiring and engaging their team, helping them see how their work contributes to the larger vision.

Behavioral Practices:

- **Communicate the vision regularly:** Reinforce the vision in team meetings, one-on-one conversations, and internal communications. The more your team hears the vision, the more it becomes ingrained in the culture.

- **Involve your team in the vision:** Encourage your team to contribute their ideas and perspectives on how to achieve the vision. This involvement increases their sense of ownership and commitment.

- **Celebrate progress:** Recognize and celebrate milestones that bring the organization closer to the vision. Celebrations not only reinforce the vision but also build momentum and motivation.

By inspiring and engaging your team, you create a sense of collective ownership over the vision, making it a central part of the organizational culture.

4. Encouraging Innovation and Risk-Taking

Visionary leaders understand that achieving a bold vision requires innovation and a willingness to take risks. They foster a culture where new ideas are encouraged, and failure is seen as a learning opportunity rather than a setback.

Behavioral Practices:

- **Create a safe environment for experimentation:** Encourage your team to explore new ideas and take calculated risks without fear of negative consequences. And that is a commitment you must make as a leader. You need to control your negative and impulsive reactions to mistakes and failures.

- **Reward innovation:** Recognize and reward employees who contribute innovative ideas or take actions that move the organization closer to its vision.

- **Learn from failures:** When something doesn't go as planned, use it as an opportunity to learn and grow. Analyze what went wrong, identify lessons learned, and apply them to future efforts.

By encouraging innovation and risk-taking, you create a dynamic and adaptable culture that is well-equipped to achieve the vision, even in the face of uncertainty.

5. Maintaining Focus and Flexibility

Visionary leaders strike a balance between staying focused on the long-term vision and being flexible enough to adapt to changing circumstances. They understand that while the vision provides direction, the path to achieving it may evolve over time.

Behavioral Practices:

- **Stay focused on the big picture:** Keep the vision front and center in your decision-making process. Avoid getting bogged down in short-term challenges that distract you as "sirens" from long-term goals.

- **Be open to change:** Recognize that the environment in which you operate is constantly changing. Be willing to adjust your strategies and approaches as needed to stay on track toward the vision. You are the first one who needs to feel comfortable with changes and embrace them.

- **Regularly review and adjust the vision:** Periodically revisit the vision to ensure it remains relevant and achievable. Make adjustments, as necessary, to reflect new information, opportunities, or challenges.

By maintaining focus and flexibility, you ensure that your vision remains a guiding force for the organization, even as the landscape around you shifts.

Science-Based Insight

Visionary thinking engages the brain's prefrontal cortex, the area responsible for planning, decision-making, and forward-thinking. When a leader effectively communicates a compelling vision, it activates this part of the brain in their employees, encouraging them to think strategically and align their actions with long-term goals.

Furthermore, a clear vision can stimulate the brain's reward system by providing a sense of purpose and direction. Dopamine, a neurotransmitter associated with motivation and pleasure, is released when individuals perceive that their work contributes to a meaningful goal. This boost in dopamine enhances focus, productivity, and overall job satisfaction, all of which are critical for building a high-performing workplace culture. By consistently reinforcing the vision, leaders can help sustain this positive neurochemical environment, driving ongoing engagement and success (Dame Leadership, 2024).

Putting pen to paper

Exercise: Crafting and Communicating Your Vision

Objective: To develop and articulate a clear, compelling vision for your team or organization that inspires and aligns everyone toward common goals.

Instructions:

1. **Reflect on your organization's core values:** Begin by identifying the core values that define your organization. Write

them down and consider how these values influence your organization's purpose and long-term goals.

2. **Identify key trends and challenges:** Consider the external and internal trends that are likely to impact your organization in the coming years. This could include market changes, technological advancements, or shifts in customer behavior. Also, think about the challenges your organization is currently facing.

3. **Envision the future:** Based on your organization's values and the trends you've identified, imagine the future you want to create. Write a brief narrative that describes what your organization will look like in 5-10 years. Be specific about the outcomes you want to achieve and how they will benefit your team, customers, and stakeholders.

4. **Define the steps to achieve your vision:** Break down your vision into actionable steps or strategic priorities. Identify what needs to happen in the short, medium, and long term to move toward this future.

5. **Craft a vision statement:** Synthesize your narrative into a concise vision statement that clearly communicates the future you envision for your organization. Ensure it is inspiring, easy to understand, and aligns with your organization's core values.

6. **Communicate your vision:** Plan how you will communicate your vision to your team. Consider different communication

channels, such as team meetings, internal newsletters, or one on-one discussions. Think about how you can reinforce the vision regularly to keep it top of mind.

7. **Gather feedback:** Share your vision with a few trusted colleagues or team members and gather their feedback. Use their input to refine your vision statement and communication plan.

8. **Implement and observe:** Begin communicating your vision to the wider team. Observe how they respond and whether their actions and attitudes begin to align with the vision. Make adjustments as needed to ensure the vision remains relevant and compelling.

Avoiding Leadership Pitfalls: The Dangers of Short-Sighted Thinking

While visionary thinking is essential for effective leadership, it's important to be aware of the pitfalls that can arise when this quality is lacking. Leaders who fail to think beyond the immediate challenges or who focus solely on short-term gains may inadvertently create a culture that is reactive, stagnant, and ultimately unsustainable.

1. Short-Term Focus and Lack of Direction

Leaders who are overly focused on short-term results may neglect the long-term vision, leading to a lack of direction and purpose within the organization. This short-sighted approach can result in a reactive rather than proactive culture, where decisions are made based on immediate needs rather than strategic goals.

Consequences:

- **Employee confusion:** Without a clear vision, employees may be unclear about their roles and how their work contributes to the organization's goals, leading to disengagement and frustration.

- **Missed opportunities:** A short-term focus may cause leaders to overlook or undervalue opportunities that could drive long-term success.

- **Burnout:** Constantly chasing short-term results can lead to employee burnout, as the organization lacks a steady direction and purpose to sustain motivation.

2. Resistance to Change and Innovation

Leaders who are resistant to change or who fail to encourage innovation may inadvertently create a culture that is stagnant and risk-averse. This can stifle creativity and prevent the organization from adapting to new challenges and opportunities.

Consequences:

- **Decreased competitiveness:** Organizations that fail to innovate may struggle to stay competitive in a rapidly changing market.

- **Low employee morale:** A lack of innovation and growth opportunities can lead to employee dissatisfaction and disengagement.

- **Increased turnover:** Employees who feel that their ideas are not valued or that the organization is resistant to change may seek opportunities elsewhere.

3. Disconnection from Organizational Values

Leaders who fail to align their vision with the organization's core values may create a disconnect between the leadership and the team. This has a chance to erode trust and weaken the organization's culture.

Consequences:

- **Erosion of trust:** When employees perceive that leadership is not aligned with the organization's values, it can lead to a breakdown of trust and credibility.

- **Cultural disintegration:** A vision that is not grounded in the organization's values can lead to a fragmented culture, where employees may feel disconnected from the mission and purpose.

- **Reduced engagement:** Employees who do not see the vision as reflective of their values and beliefs are less likely to be engaged and committed to the organization's success.

Conclusion: Visionary Thinking as the Compass for Leadership

Visionary thinking is not just about imagining the future; it's about shaping it. As a leader, your vision serves as the compass that guides your organization through uncharted waters, providing direction, inspiration, and purpose. By cultivating a visionary mindset and translating it into actionable behaviors, you can create a workplace culture that is dynamic, resilient, and driven by a shared commitment to a brighter future.

In this chapter, we've explored how visionary thinking influences leadership and organizational culture. We've discussed the mindset necessary for visionary leadership, the behaviors that bring it to life, and the potential ripple effects it can have on the organization as a whole. We've also examined the potential pitfalls of short-sighted thinking and the importance of staying focused on the long-term vision.

As you continue your leadership journey, remember that what you see is how you lead. By leading with visionary thinking, you not only chart a course for the future but also inspire your team to follow you on that journey with passion, dedication, and a shared sense of purpose.

Practice Nr. 3: Transparency and Open Communication

Transparency and open communication are the bedrock of any high-performing organizational culture. Without them, misunderstandings flourish, trust erodes, and teams struggle to function effectively. Leaders who prioritize transparency and foster open communication create an environment where trust is built, ideas are shared freely, and everyone feels informed and engaged.

In this chapter of *The Mirror Effect: What You See, Is How You Lead!*, we will delve into the importance of transparency and open communication in leadership. We will explore the mindset needed to embrace these principles and the behaviors that reinforce them, ensuring that your team operates with clarity, trust, and mutual respect. Additionally, we will examine the neurological impact of transparency and communication on employee engagement and morale.

M. was the CEO of a mid-sized manufacturing company. He was known for his strategic decision-making and his ability to keep the company on a steady course. However, he was also someone who believed in shielding his team from the more challenging aspects of running the business, thinking that by doing so, he was keeping them focused and undistracted. Unfortunately, this lack of transparency began to create significant issues.

The company was facing a serious crisis: a major client was considering terminating a contract due to repeated delays in production. M. knew that losing this client could have disastrous financial consequences. He spent countless hours behind closed doors, negotiating with the client and trying to fix the production issues, but he chose not to inform his team about the situation. He feared that revealing the problem might cause panic and demotivate them.

One day, during a routine team meeting, the Head of Production raised concerns about the increasing pressure and sudden changes in production schedules. "M.," she asked, "why the sudden urgency? The team is feeling the strain, and it's affecting our performance. What's going on?"

M., still intent on keeping the problem to himself, responded vaguely. "We just need to stay competitive," he said, avoiding eye contact. "Let's focus on meeting these deadlines. It's important for our long-term success."

The Head of Production looked unconvinced, but she didn't press further. The rest of the team, however, left the meeting with growing unease. The vague answers and increased pressure led to speculation and rumors. Was the company in financial trouble? Were there going to be layoffs? The lack of clear communication began to erode trust, and morale plummeted. Productivity dropped, and a once cohesive team started to feel disconnected and anxious.

Recognizing that something was deeply wrong, M. reached out to me for advice. During our conversation, I asked, "M., why haven't you shared the full situation with your team?"

He hesitated, then admitted, "I didn't want to worry them. I thought it was better to manage the crisis myself and keep them focused on their work."

"But how has that worked out?" I gently asked.

M. sighed, rubbing his forehead. "Not well. They're stressed, there's a lot of speculation, and I can feel that they don't trust me the way they used to."

"That's because trust is built on transparency and open communication," I explained. "When you withhold information, even with good intentions, you create a gap that people will fill with their own fears and assumptions. By not being transparent, you've inadvertently undermined the very thing you were trying to protect—their focus and trust in you as a leader."

M. looked pensive. "So, what do I do now?"

"Start by being honest," I advised. "Call a meeting, explain the situation clearly, and involve them in the solution. Let them know that you trust them to handle the truth and that you value their input in overcoming this challenge."

The following day, M. gathered his leadership team. This time, he was direct. "I need to be honest with you all," he began, taking a deep breath. "We're facing a serious issue with one of our major clients. They're considering ending our contract due to delays in production, and I've been trying to resolve it on my own. But I realize now that I've made a mistake by not bringing you into the loop sooner."

The room was silent, but instead of the panic M. feared, he saw concern mixed with determination in his team's eyes. He continued, "I trust each of you to help us navigate through this. I believe that together, we can find a solution."

To M's relief, the team responded positively. Sarah spoke up, "Thank you for telling us, M. We can work through this, but we need to know what we're up against. Let's figure out how to get production back on track."

The team rallied together, brainstorming ideas and coming up with a plan to address the production issues. They also devised a strategy to communicate more effectively with the client, which eventually helped salvage the contract. The crisis wasn't easy to manage, but M's decision to be transparent and involve his team in the process restored the trust that had been shaken.

Reflecting on the experience, M. realized that transparency and open communication weren't just nice-to-haves—they were essential foundations of trust. By being honest and open with his team, he not only resolved the immediate crisis but also strengthened the bonds within the team, fostering a more resilient and committed workforce. He learned that leadership isn't just about making decisions; it's about building trust through clear, honest, and open communication, especially during the most challenging times.

Understanding Transparency and Open Communication in Leadership

Transparency in leadership means being open and honest about decisions, processes, and challenges. It involves sharing relevant information with your team, even when the news is difficult or the future is uncertain. Open communication, on the other hand, is about creating a two-way flow of information where ideas, feedback, and concerns can be shared freely without fear of retribution or judgment.

When leaders prioritize transparency and open communication, they set the stage for a culture of trust and collaboration. Employees are more likely to feel valued and respected when they are kept in the loop and when their voices are heard. This, in turn, leads to higher engagement, better decision-making, and a stronger sense of ownership and accountability across the organization.

The Mindset of a Transparent and Communicative Leader

To lead with transparency and open communication, you must first adopt a mindset that values honesty, inclusivity, and trust. This mindset encourages you to be forthright with information and to create an environment where everyone feels comfortable sharing their thoughts and ideas.

1. Valuing Honesty and Integrity

A transparent leader believes that honesty is the best policy, even when the truth is difficult to share. They understand that integrity is the foundation of trust and that being open and honest with their team fosters a culture of respect and accountability.

Mindset: Embrace the idea that transparency, even in challenging situations, builds credibility and trust. Understand that honesty and integrity are essential for creating a workplace where employees feel secure and valued.

2. Embracing Vulnerability

Transparency often requires vulnerability—admitting when you don't have all the answers, when mistakes are made, or when the organization is facing difficulties. Leaders who embrace vulnerability demonstrate that it's okay to be human and that openness is more important than maintaining a façade of perfection.

Mindset: Recognize that vulnerability is a strength, not a weakness. By being open about your own challenges and uncertainties, you encourage your team to do the same, fostering a culture of mutual support and understanding.

3. Prioritizing Inclusivity and Openness

A leader who values open communication understands that every voice matters. They prioritize inclusivity by creating channels for all team members to share their ideas, feedback, and concerns. This inclusivity ensures that decisions are informed by diverse perspectives and that everyone feels heard.

Mindset: Believe that the best ideas and solutions come from a diversity of voices. Commit to creating an environment where open communication is encouraged and where all team members feel comfortable contributing.

4. Fostering a Culture of Trust

Transparency and open communication are integral to building trust within an organization. Leaders who value these principles understand that trust is earned through consistent, honest, and open interactions. They know that trust is fragile and must be nurtured through every communication and decision.

Mindset: Understand that trust is the foundation of a strong organizational culture. Commit to being transparent in your actions and communications, and work to build and maintain trust with your team at all times.

Behavioral Practices for Leading with Transparency and Open Communication

Once you have cultivated a mindset that values transparency and open communication, the next step is to translate that mindset into behaviors that reinforce these principles within your team. These behaviors are crucial for creating a culture where trust is built, information flows freely, and everyone feels included and valued.

1. Sharing Information Openly and Regularly

Transparency starts with sharing information openly and regularly with your team. This includes not only good news but also challenges, changes, and uncertainties. By keeping your team informed, you demonstrate that you trust them and that you value their input.

Behavioral Practices:

- **Regular updates:** Provide your team with regular updates on organizational goals, progress, and any changes that may impact their work. Use team meetings, newsletters, or digital platforms to share this information consistently.

- **Be open about challenges:** Don't shy away from sharing difficult news or challenges the organization is facing. When you're transparent about challenges, you invite your team to be part of the solution, which can foster a stronger sense of ownership and collaboration.

- **Explain decisions:** When decisions are made, especially those that affect the team, take the time to explain the reasoning behind them. This helps employees understand the bigger picture and feel more connected to the organization's direction.

By sharing information openly and regularly, you build a culture of trust and transparency where employees feel informed and engaged.

2. Encouraging Open Dialogue and Feedback

Open communication is a two-way street. It's not just about sharing information with your team; it's also about creating opportunities for them to share their thoughts, ideas, and concerns with you. Leaders who encourage open dialogue foster a culture where everyone feels comfortable speaking up.

Behavioral Practices:

- **Open-door policy:** Establish an open-door policy that encourages employees to come to you with their ideas, feedback, or concerns. Make it clear that their input is valued and will be taken seriously.

- **Regular check-ins:** Hold regular one-on-one check-ins with team members to discuss their progress, challenges, and any feedback they may have. Use these meetings as an opportunity to listen and learn from their experiences.

- **Anonymous feedback options:** Provide channels for anonymous feedback, such as suggestion boxes or digital surveys. This ensures that employees who may be hesitant to speak up in person still have a voice.

By encouraging open dialogue and feedback, you create a culture of inclusivity and collaboration where every team member feels valued and heard.

3. Modeling Transparent Behavior

Leaders set the tone for the entire organization. If you want your team to be transparent and open in their communication, you must model these behaviors yourself. This includes being honest about your own challenges, admitting when you don't have all the answers, and being willing to have difficult conversations.

Behavioral Practices:

- **Admit mistakes:** When you make a mistake, own up to it and discuss what you've learned from the experience. This sets an example for your team and encourages them to be open about their own mistakes.

- **Be open about uncertainties:** If there are areas where the future is uncertain or where you don't have all the answers, be honest about it. Transparency in these moments builds trust and shows your team that it's okay to be unsure.

- **Have difficult conversations:** Don't avoid difficult conversations or tough topics. Address them head-on with honesty and compassion, and encourage your team to do the same.

By modeling transparent behavior, you create a culture where openness and honesty are the norm, not the exception.

4. Building Trust Through Consistent Communication

Transparency and open communication are most effective when they are consistent. Leaders who communicate regularly and reliably build trust with their team, as employees know they can count on their leader to keep them informed and involved.

Behavioral Practices:

- **Consistency in communication:** Ensure that you communicate with your team consistently, whether through regular meetings, updates, or check-ins. Consistency builds trust and ensures that your team feels connected and informed.

- **Follow through on commitments:** If you commit to sharing information or providing updates, follow through. Consistency in your actions reinforces the trust you've built through your communication.

- **Be responsive:** Respond to questions, concerns, and feedback in a timely manner. This shows your team that their input is important and that you are committed to maintaining open lines of communication.

By building trust through consistent communication, you reinforce a culture of transparency and reliability, where employees feel secure and confident in their roles.

Science-Based Insight

Research in neuroscience has shown that transparency and open communication in leadership can significantly impact how employees' brains function, particularly in areas related to trust, motivation, and emotional well-being. The brain's prefrontal cortex, responsible for decision-making and social behavior, plays a key role in how we perceive trust and transparency in others.

When leaders communicate openly and transparently, it activates the brain's oxytocin system, often referred to as the "trust hormone." Oxytocin is associated with feelings of trust, bonding, and emotional safety. When employees perceive their leaders as trustworthy and transparent, their brains release oxytocin, which enhances their sense of connection, loyalty, and commitment to the organization (Baumgartner et al., 2008).

Moreover, open communication reduces the brain's stress response, particularly in the amygdala, which is involved in processing fear and anxiety. When employees are kept informed and feel that their voices are heard, it lowers their cortisol levels, the hormone associated with stress. This reduction in stress leads to better focus, higher productivity, and a more positive workplace atmosphere (Baumgartner et al., 2008; Ross, 2024).

By fostering transparency and open communication, leaders can create a neurochemical environment that promotes trust, reduces stress, and enhances overall job satisfaction, all of which are critical for building a high-performing workplace culture.

Putting pen to paper

Exercise: The Open Communication Audit

Objective: To assess and enhance the level of transparency and open communication within your team or organization by identifying areas for improvement and implementing practical strategies.

Instructions:

1. **Conduct a communication audit:** Start by assessing the current state of communication within your team or organization. Reflect on the following questions:

   - How often do you communicate important information to your team?

   - Do your team members feel comfortable sharing their ideas, feedback, or concerns?

   - Are there any barriers to open communication, such as fear of retribution, lack of time, or hierarchical structures?

   - How transparent are you about challenges, changes, and decisions?

2. **Gather feedback from your team:** Use anonymous surveys, one-on-one meetings, or team discussions to gather feedback on how your team perceives the current level of transparency and communication. Ask them to identify any gaps or areas where they feel communication could be improved.

3. **Identify areas for improvement:** Based on your audit and the feedback you've gathered, identify specific areas where transparency and open communication could be enhanced. This could include more regular updates, creating new communication channels, or encouraging more open dialogue.

4. **Develop an action plan:** Create a plan to address the areas for improvement you've identified. This could involve:

   - Setting up regular team meetings or newsletters to keep everyone informed.

   - Establishing an open-door policy to encourage more open communication.

   - Providing training or workshops on effective communication for your team.

   - Implementing anonymous feedback channels to ensure all voices are heard.

5. **Implement and observe:** Put your action plan into practice and observe the impact on your team's communication and overall culture. Pay attention to how your team responds and

whether there is an increase in trust, collaboration, and engagement.

6. **Reflect and adjust:** After a few weeks or months, reflect on the changes you've implemented and gather feedback from your team again. Use this feedback to make any necessary adjustments and continue to build a culture of transparency and open communication.

By regularly auditing and improving your communication practices, you can ensure that transparency and open communication remain central to your leadership approach, fostering a high-performing and trust-filled workplace culture.

Avoiding Leadership Pitfalls: The Dangers of Secrecy and Poor Communication

While transparency and open communication are essential for effective leadership, it's important to recognize the pitfalls of their absence. Leaders who fail to communicate openly or who withhold information can create a culture of mistrust, confusion, and disengagement.

1. Lack of Transparency and Erosion of Trust

Leaders who withhold information or fail to communicate openly risk eroding trust within their organization. When employees feel that they are being kept in the dark, they may become suspicious, disengaged, and less committed to their work.

Consequences:

- **Decreased morale:** A lack of transparency can lead to decreased morale, as employees feel undervalued and disconnected from the organization's goals.

- **Higher turnover:** When trust is eroded, employees are more likely to leave the organization in search of a workplace where they feel more valued and informed.

- **Reduced collaboration:** A lack of transparency can lead to silos and reduced collaboration, as employees become hesitant to share information or ideas.

2. Poor Communication and Increased Misunderstandings

Leaders who fail to communicate effectively can create confusion and misunderstandings within their team. Without clear and open communication, employees may struggle to understand their roles, responsibilities, and the organization's direction.

Consequences:

- **Lower productivity:** Poor communication can lead to lower productivity, as employees may not have the information they need to perform their jobs effectively.

- **Increased conflict:** Misunderstandings and miscommunication can lead to increased conflict within the team as employees become frustrated or confused.

- **Missed opportunities:** A lack of open communication can result in missed opportunities for collaboration, innovation, and growth.

3. Secrecy and Fear-Based Cultures

Leaders who operate in secrecy or who discourage open communication can create a fear-based culture where employees are afraid to speak up. This can stifle creativity, innovation, and engagement, leading to a toxic work environment.

Consequences:

- **Decreased creativity:** In a fear-based culture, employees may be reluctant to share their ideas or take risks, leading to decreased creativity and innovation.

- **High-stress levels:** A culture of secrecy and fear can lead to high levels of stress and anxiety, as employees feel uncertain about their future and their roles.

- **Negative workplace culture:** Secrecy and poor communication can contribute to a negative workplace culture, where trust is low, and disengagement is high.

Conclusion: Transparency and Open Communication as Pillars of Leadership

Transparency and open communication are not just leadership strategies; they are pillars that support the entire structure of your organizational culture. By leading with transparency, you build trust.

By fostering open communication, you create an environment where ideas flourish, challenges are addressed, and everyone feels valued and informed.

In this chapter, we've explored how transparency and open communication influence leadership and organizational culture. We've discussed the mindset necessary to embrace these principles, the behaviors that bring them to life, and the ripple effects they have on the organization as a whole. We've also examined the potential pitfalls of secrecy and poor communication and the importance of maintaining openness and honesty in all interactions.

As you continue your leadership journey, remember that what you see is how you lead. By leading with transparency and open communication, you not only strengthen your team but also lay the foundation for a high-performing, resilient, and trust-filled workplace culture.

In the chapters that follow, we will explore additional cognitive and behavioral practices that will help you refine your leadership approach and create a thriving, high-performing organizational culture. Together, we will uncover the full spectrum of leadership qualities that will empower you to lead with confidence, clarity, and authenticity.

Practice Nr. 4: Inclusivity
and Diversity Appreciation

Inclusivity and diversity are often discussed in the context of fairness and equality, but their importance in leadership goes far beyond these foundational principles. When leaders actively appreciate and promote inclusivity and diversity, they unlock a wellspring of creativity, innovation, and resilience within their organizations. A culture that values diverse perspectives fosters an environment where all employees feel valued, engaged, and empowered to contribute their best.

In this chapter of *The Mirror Effect: What You See, Is How You Lead!*, we will explore how inclusivity and diversity appreciation shape organizational culture and drive success. We will examine the mindset necessary to embrace these principles fully and the behaviors that make inclusivity and diversity a lived reality within your team. Additionally, we will delve into the neurological and psychological impact of inclusivity on employee engagement, creativity, and overall workplace harmony.

I once worked with a leader named J., the manager of a department in a wholesale store. J. was good at his job, managing inventory, sales targets, and keeping operations smooth. His team was generally productive and efficient, but there was one issue that J. had been ignoring for some time— one of his team members, L., was often isolated from the rest of the group. J. and the other team members considered L. "different"—some described her as "weird"—because she didn't socialize much and had a different way of approaching tasks compared to everyone else.

L. was methodical, organized, and quiet, preferring to work alone and follow her own processes for completing tasks. While she was diligent and her work was always accurate, J. noticed that the other team members didn't engage with her much. They would huddle together for lunch and coffee breaks, excluding L., and often didn't ask for her input during meetings. J., rather than addressing the situation, kept his distance, too. He assumed L. preferred to be left alone and thought, "She's different, but as long as the work gets done, it's not my problem."

One day, during a busy holiday season, the team was working on a particularly challenging inventory issue. They couldn't keep up with customer demand, and the standard processes weren't working efficiently enough. Despite the mounting pressure, no one considered asking L. for her ideas. J., feeling the stress, gathered the team for an urgent meeting to find a solution. The same few voices dominated the discussion, and they proposed tweaking their usual method slightly, but J. knew it wouldn't be enough to handle the volume.

L., who had been quietly listening, finally spoke up. "I've been working on a new inventory tracking method on my own time. It might seem unconventional, but I think it could help us process orders faster and with fewer errors, especially during peak periods like this."

The room went silent. J., surprised that L. had spoken up, was hesitant. In the past, he had dismissed her suggestions as "out-of-the-box" and didn't want to risk trying something new under pressure. But in that moment, he remembered something from our coaching sessions: the importance of appreciating diversity, not just in background or identity, but in thinking and approaches.

Feeling a shift, J. decided to embrace inclusivity rather than dismiss L.'s ideas. "L.," he said, "can you walk us through your process? Let's hear what you've been working on."

L., though a bit nervous, began explaining her system. It was more efficient, used fewer resources, and integrated better with their updated inventory software. It was clear she had put a lot of thought into it. J. noticed some of the team members exchanging glances, but he pressed on, asking her questions and encouraging others to weigh in. Slowly, the team realized that her method made sense, and they began to ask her how they could implement it quickly.

The next day, with J.'s support, the team tested L.'s system, and to their surprise, it worked even better than expected. They were able to process the holiday orders more efficiently than in previous years, reducing customer complaints and improving team productivity.

After the success, J. realized how wrong he had been to overlook L.'s potential simply because she didn't fit into the typical mold of what he and the rest of the team were comfortable with. Her different approach—what they had seen as "weird"—turned out to be the very thing that solved their biggest problem. By embracing inclusivity and valuing diversity in thinking, J. had unlocked a new level of performance within his team.

To address the underlying issues, J. organized a team meeting, not about work but about how they interacted with each other. "We've been missing out on some great ideas because we haven't appreciated all the different strengths each of us brings to the table," he admitted. "I know I haven't done enough to foster an inclusive environment, and that's on me. From now on, we're going to do better. I want everyone to feel like their voice matters and that they can contribute in ways that make the whole team better."

The team started to make changes, too. They began inviting L. to join them during breaks and included her in conversations. Slowly, the social barriers began to break down, and L., feeling more accepted, started participating more in discussions. The overall team dynamic improved, and the department saw higher engagement and more innovative ideas flowing from everyone.

Reflecting on the experience, J. learned that inclusivity and diversity aren't just about filling quotas or meeting HR requirements—they're about recognizing the value of different perspectives, approaches, and ways of thinking. When leaders make an effort to include and appreciate all team members, they unlock creativity, drive innovation, and foster a stronger sense of unity within their teams.

By valuing L.'s unique approach, J. not only solved an immediate problem but also transformed his department into a more inclusive, innovative, and connected team. He learned that true leadership involves seeing beyond surface-level differences and appreciating the diversity that each team member brings to the table. In doing so, he created a culture where everyone could thrive.

Understanding Inclusivity and Diversity in Leadership

Inclusivity in leadership means creating an environment where all team members feel respected, valued, and empowered to contribute, regardless of their background, identity, or perspective. Diversity, meanwhile, refers to the presence of differences within a team, including but not limited to race, gender, age, sexual orientation, religion, and cognitive styles.

When leaders prioritize inclusivity and diversity, they create a culture where differences are not just tolerated but celebrated as strengths. This inclusive culture leads to more innovative solutions, better decision-making, and a stronger sense of unity within the organization. By recognizing and leveraging the unique perspectives of each team member, leaders can build a more resilient and high-performing organization.

The Mindset of an Inclusive and Diversity-Appreciative Leader

To lead with inclusivity and diversity appreciation, you must first cultivate a mindset that values and actively seeks out diverse perspectives. This mindset goes beyond simply acknowledging differences; it involves understanding the power of diversity and committing to creating an environment where everyone can thrive.

1. Valuing Diversity as a Strength

An inclusive leader sees diversity as a strength, not a challenge. They understand that different perspectives lead to more creative solutions and that a diverse team is better equipped to handle complex problems.

Mindset: Embrace the idea that diversity enhances the organization's ability to innovate, adapt, and grow. Understand that by bringing together people with different backgrounds and perspectives, you create a richer and more dynamic team.

2. Prioritizing Equity and Fairness

Inclusive leaders are committed to ensuring that all team members have equal access to opportunities, resources, and support. They recognize that equity is essential for creating a level playing field where everyone can contribute to their fullest potential.

Mindset: Believe in the importance of equity and fairness in the workplace. Recognize that true inclusivity involves actively addressing barriers and biases that may prevent certain individuals or groups from fully participating.

3. Embracing Cultural Humility

Cultural humility is the recognition that we all have biases and limitations in our understanding of others' experiences. Inclusive leaders approach diversity with humility, acknowledging that they have much to learn from the diverse perspectives of their team members.

Mindset: Cultivate an attitude of curiosity and openness towards others' experiences and viewpoints. Be willing to learn, listen, and adapt your thinking based on the insights of those who are different from you.

4. Committing to Continuous Improvement

Inclusivity and diversity are not one-time achievements but ongoing processes. Inclusive leaders are committed to continuously improving their understanding of diversity and their ability to create an inclusive environment.

Mindset: Recognize that inclusivity is a journey, not a destination. Commit to ongoing learning, self-reflection, and adaptation as you work to create a more inclusive and diverse workplace.

Behavioral Practices for Leading with Inclusivity and Diversity Appreciation

Once you have cultivated an inclusive and diversity-appreciative mindset, the next step is to translate that mindset into behaviors that actively promote and reinforce these values within your team. These behaviors are crucial for creating a culture where everyone feels included, valued, and empowered to contribute their best.

1. Actively Seeking Diverse Perspectives

Inclusive leaders make a conscious effort to seek out and incorporate diverse perspectives in decision-making processes. They understand that the best solutions often come from considering a wide range of viewpoints.

Behavioral Practices:

- **Diverse teams:** When forming teams for projects or initiatives, intentionally include individuals with different backgrounds, experiences, and perspectives.

- **Encourage participation:** In meetings and discussions, actively encourage participation from all team members, especially those who may be less likely to speak up.

- **Seek feedback:** Regularly seek feedback from a diverse cross-section of your team on decisions, policies, and initiatives. Use this feedback to inform your actions and strategies.

By actively seeking diverse perspectives, you create a culture where all voices are heard and where diverse viewpoints are valued and leveraged for better decision-making.

2. Providing Equal Opportunities and Resources

Inclusive leaders ensure that all team members have equal access to opportunities, resources, and support. They recognize and address systemic barriers that may disadvantage certain groups and work to create a level playing field for everyone.

Behavioral Practices:

- **Equitable resource allocation:** Ensure that resources, such as training, mentorship, and career development opportunities, are distributed equitably across the team.

- **Address biases:** Be proactive in identifying and addressing biases in hiring, promotion, and evaluation processes. Implement policies and practices that promote equity and fairness.

- **Support underrepresented groups:** Provide additional support and resources to individuals from underrepresented or marginalized groups to ensure they have the tools they need to succeed.

By providing equal opportunities and resources, you create an environment where everyone has the chance to thrive and contribute to their fullest potential.

3. Fostering a Culture of Respect and Inclusion

Inclusive leaders foster a culture where respect and inclusion are the norm. They create an environment where differences are celebrated and where all team members feel safe, valued, and respected.

Behavioral Practices:

- **Model respectful behavior:** Demonstrate respect for all team members in your words and actions. Address any instances of disrespect or exclusion promptly and appropriately.

- **Promote inclusive language:** Encourage the use of inclusive language in all communications, both formal and informal. Ensure that all team members are aware of and adhere to these standards.

- **Celebrate diversity:** Recognize and celebrate the diverse backgrounds, cultures, and experiences of your team members through events, discussions, and acknowledgments.

By fostering a culture of respect and inclusion, you create a workplace where everyone feels valued and empowered to contribute their best.

4. Committing to Continuous Learning and Improvement

Inclusivity and diversity appreciation require ongoing effort and commitment. Inclusive leaders are dedicated to continuously learning about diversity and improving their ability to create an inclusive environment.

Behavioral Practices:

- **Participate in diversity training:** Engage in regular diversity, equity, and inclusion (DEI) training to enhance your understanding of these issues and to develop new strategies for fostering inclusivity.

- **Encourage learning for your team:** Promote diversity and inclusion training for all team members and provide opportunities for ongoing learning and development in these areas.

- **Reflect and adapt:** Regularly reflect on your own behaviors, biases, and assumptions. Be open to feedback and willing to adapt your leadership approach based on what you learn.

By committing to continuous learning and improvement, you ensure that inclusivity and diversity remain central to your leadership approach and that your team continues to grow and thrive in these areas.

Science-Based Insight

Recent research from neuroscience emphasizes that a diverse and inclusive environment not only fosters creativity and innovation but also significantly impacts the brain's emotional and cognitive functioning.

When individuals are exposed to diverse perspectives and ideas, it stimulates divergent thinking, which is the ability to generate multiple, creative solutions to problems. This process activates the prefrontal cortex, a region responsible for complex problem-solving and cognitive flexibility. The interaction of diverse team members encourages broader thinking, which enhances innovation and creativity (Frontiers in Psychology, 2020).

Additionally, inclusivity plays a critical role in activating the limbic system, particularly the amygdala and ventral striatum, which regulate emotions such as belonging and trust. When team members feel included and valued, their brains release oxytocin, the hormone associated with trust and bonding. This neurochemical response leads to stronger team cohesion, higher engagement, and increased commitment to organizational goals (Bartz et al., 2011; Frontiers, 2020).

By fostering an inclusive environment, leaders create the neurochemical conditions necessary for enhancing creativity, collaboration, and emotional well-being, all of which contribute to building a high-performing and innovative workplace culture.

Putting pen to paper

Exercise: The Diversity and Inclusion Assessment

Objective: To assess the current state of inclusivity and diversity within your team or organization and to develop strategies for enhancing these values in your leadership and workplace culture.

Instructions:

1. **Conduct a diversity and inclusion assessment:** Begin by assessing the current state of diversity and inclusion within your team or organization. Reflect on the following questions:

   - What is the demographic composition of your team in terms of race, gender, age, background, and experiences?

   - How inclusive is the culture within your team? Do all members feel valued, respected, and included?

   - Are there any barriers or biases that may prevent certain individuals or groups from fully participating or advancing within the organization?

   - How are diverse perspectives currently incorporated into decision-making processes?

2. **Gather feedback from your team:** Use anonymous surveys, one-on-one meetings, or focus groups to gather feedback from your team on their perceptions of diversity and inclusion. Ask them to identify any areas where they feel inclusivity could be improved.

3. **Identify strengths and areas for improvement:** Based on your assessment and the feedback you've gathered, identify the strengths and areas for improvement in your team's approach to diversity and inclusion. Consider what's working well and what could be enhanced.

4. **Develop an action plan:** Create a plan to address the areas for improvement you've identified. This could involve:

   - Implementing initiatives to recruit and retain a more diverse workforce.

   - Providing diversity, equity, and inclusion (DEI) training for yourself and your team.

   - Creating channels for diverse perspectives to be heard and incorporated into decision-making and problem-solving.

5. **Implement and observe:** Put your action plan into practice and observe the impact on your team's inclusivity and overall culture. Pay attention to how your team responds and whether there is an increase in engagement, collaboration, and innovation.

6. **Reflect and adjust:** After a few months, reflect on the changes you've implemented and gather feedback from your team again. Use this feedback to make any necessary adjustments and to continue building a culture of inclusivity and diversity.

By regularly assessing and improving your approach to inclusivity and diversity, you can ensure that these values remain central to your leadership approach, fostering a high-performing, innovative, and united workplace culture.

Avoiding Leadership Pitfalls:
The Dangers of Homogeneity and Exclusion

While inclusivity and diversity are essential for effective leadership, it's important to recognize the pitfalls of their absence. Leaders who fail to promote diversity or who allow exclusionary practices to persist can create a culture that is stagnant, divided, and ultimately less effective.

1. Homogeneity and Groupthink

Leaders who prioritize similarity over diversity may inadvertently create a homogeneous culture where groupthink prevails. In such environments, teams may be less likely to challenge the status quo, leading to stagnation and missed opportunities for innovation.

Consequences:

- **Decreased creativity:** Homogeneous teams are less likely to generate creative ideas or innovative solutions, as they may be more prone to groupthink and less likely to challenge assumptions.

- **Reduced adaptability:** A lack of diversity can make it harder for the organization to adapt to change, as the team may lack the diverse perspectives needed to navigate new challenges.

- **Lower performance:** Homogeneous teams may be less effective in problem-solving and decision-making, leading to lower overall performance.

2. Exclusion and Disengagement

Leaders who fail to create an inclusive environment risk alienating certain individuals or groups, leading to disengagement and a lack of participation. Exclusion can occur when certain voices are ignored, marginalized, or undervalued, leading to a culture of division and discontent.

Consequences:

- **Decreased morale:** Exclusion leads to lower morale among those who feel marginalized or undervalued, reducing their motivation and commitment to the organization.

- **Higher turnover:** Employees who feel excluded or unsupported are more likely to leave the organization in search of a more inclusive and respectful workplace.

- **Negative workplace culture:** A culture of exclusion can lead to division, conflict, and a toxic work environment where trust and collaboration are eroded.

3. Inequity and Unfairness

Leaders who fail to address systemic biases and barriers may perpetuate inequities within the organization, leading to unfair treatment of certain individuals or groups. Inequity can manifest in disparities in pay, opportunities, resources, and support, leading to resentment and dissatisfaction.

Consequences:

- **Decreased trust:** Inequity undermines trust within the organization, as employees perceive that the system is unfair or biased.

- **Reduced engagement:** Employees who feel that they are not being treated fairly are less likely to be engaged in their work, leading to lower productivity and job satisfaction.

- **Legal and reputational risks:** Inequity and unfair practices can lead to legal challenges and damage the organization's reputation, making it harder to attract and retain talent.

Conclusion: Inclusivity and Diversity as Catalysts for Leadership and Organizational Success

Inclusivity and diversity are not just buzzwords; they are essential components of effective leadership and organizational success. By leading with inclusivity and diversity appreciation, you create a culture where differences are celebrated, voices are heard, and everyone feels empowered to contribute their best.

In this chapter, we've explored how inclusivity and diversity influence leadership and organizational culture. We've discussed the mindset necessary to embrace these principles fully, the behaviors that bring them to life, and the ripple effects they have on the organization as a whole. We've also examined the potential pitfalls of homogeneity and exclusion and the importance of maintaining inclusivity and fairness in all interactions.

As you continue your leadership journey, remember that what you see is how you lead. By leading with inclusivity and diversity appreciation, you not only strengthen your team but also lay the foundation for a high-performing, innovative, and unified workplace culture.

In the chapters that follow, we will explore additional cognitive and behavioral practices that will help you refine your leadership approach and create a thriving, high-performing organizational culture. Together, we will uncover the full spectrum of leadership qualities that will empower you to lead with confidence, clarity, and inclusivity.

Practice Nr. 5: Resilience and Adaptability

In today's fast-paced and ever-changing world, the ability to be resilient and adaptable is not just a desirable trait for leaders—it's essential. Organizations that thrive in the face of uncertainty and change are those led by individuals who can maintain composure, learn from setbacks, and adjust their strategies as needed. Resilient and adaptable leaders inspire their teams to embrace change, overcome challenges, and continually grow stronger together.

In this chapter of *The Mirror Effect: What You See, Is How You Lead!*, we will explore the importance of resilience and adaptability in leadership. We will examine the mindset required to cultivate these qualities and the behaviors that foster a resilient and adaptable culture within your team. Additionally, we will delve into the neurological and psychological impact of resilience and adaptability on employee engagement, performance, and well-being.

M. was the Commercial Manager of a well-established consumer goods company. M. had been with the company for over a decade and had seen it grow from a small operation into a market leader. He was deeply familiar with the company's traditional sales strategies and prided himself on his ability to maintain strong relationships with long-standing clients. M. was a steady and reliable leader known for his consistency and commitment to proven methods. However, when the company decided to implement a new, more aggressive digital strategy, M. found himself struggling to adapt.

The company's leadership, recognizing the shift in consumer behavior toward online shopping, decided to pivot from its traditional brick-and-mortar focus to a more digital-oriented approach. This new strategy included launching e-commerce platforms, utilizing data analytics to personalize marketing, and investing in social media to reach younger consumers. For M., who had built his career on face-to-face relationships and traditional sales channels, this new direction felt foreign and uncomfortable.

During a meeting where the new strategy was rolled out, M. listened in silence as the CEO and other executives enthusiastically discussed the potential of digital marketing and e-commerce. They presented data showing the rapid growth of online sales and the increasing importance of a strong digital presence. While his colleagues seemed excited, M. couldn't shake his doubts. He had always believed that personal relationships and in-store experiences were the keys to success.

As the meeting ended, he felt overwhelmed and resistant to the changes.

Over the following weeks, M. struggled to implement the new strategy within his team. He continued to push for traditional methods, urging his sales team to focus on in-person meetings and maintaining their usual accounts. However, he began to notice that while his team was working hard, they weren't achieving the same results as before. Meanwhile, other departments that had embraced the digital approach were seeing early successes. The tension grew as M.'s team fell behind in the company's new key performance indicators.

Realizing that he was at a crossroads, M. reached out to me for guidance. During our conversation, I asked him, "M., what's holding you back from fully embracing the new strategy?"

He sighed, clearly frustrated. "I've been in this business for a long time, and I know what works. This new digital approach feels like it's moving away from what has always made us successful. I'm worried that we're losing the personal touch that our clients value."

"I understand," I replied. "But consider this: the market is changing, and consumer behavior is evolving rapidly. What worked in the past may not be enough to keep you competitive in the future. The key to thriving in this environment is adaptability—being willing to learn new skills and approaches, even when they challenge your comfort zone. How might you start seeing this new strategy as an opportunity rather than a threat?"

M. was quiet for a moment, then admitted, "I guess I'm afraid of losing control, of not being as effective in a digital world as I was in the traditional one."

"Change can be daunting," I acknowledged. "But resilience isn't just about sticking to what you know; it's about being open to growth and learning. You've built a strong foundation—now it's time to expand on that by embracing the new tools and strategies at your disposal. What if you approached this new strategy not as a replacement for your skills but as an enhancement?"

M. nodded slowly. "I hadn't thought of it that way. But where do I start?"

"Start by educating yourself and your team," I suggested. "Take the time to learn about digital marketing and e-commerce. Partner with colleagues who have experience in these areas and see how you can integrate these new strategies with your existing strengths. Show your team that you're committed to this new direction and that you're willing to lead by example."

The next day, M. gathered his team and addressed them with a newfound determination. "I know this new strategy has been challenging for all of us," he began. "But I've realized that we need to adapt if we want to continue succeeding in this changing market. I'm committed to learning everything I can about our digital strategy, and I want us to embrace these changes together. Let's figure out how we can blend our traditional strengths with these new opportunities."

M. then took the initiative to partner with the company's digital marketing team, attending training sessions and encouraging his team to do the same. He also began experimenting with online sales strategies, using data analytics to better understand customer preferences and adjusting his team's approach accordingly. Slowly but surely, his team started to see results. They were able to reach new customers through online channels while maintaining strong relationships with their existing clients.

Over time, M. became a vocal advocate for the company's digital strategy, sharing his success stories with other departments and helping to lead the company's transformation. The company not only survived the shift in consumer behavior but thrived, capturing new market segments and solidifying its position as a leader in the industry.

Reflecting on the experience, M. realized that resilience and adaptability were not just about weathering change—they were about embracing it. By letting go of his initial resistance and choosing to learn and grow, he was able to lead his team through a challenging transition and emerge stronger on the other side. M. learned that true leadership requires the courage to adapt, the willingness to explore new paths, and the ability to see change as an opportunity for innovation and growth.

Understanding Resilience and Adaptability in Leadership

Resilience in leadership refers to the ability to recover from setbacks, stay positive under pressure, and continue moving forward despite challenges. It's about maintaining a strong sense of purpose and focus even in the face of adversity. Adaptability, on the other hand, is the ability to adjust to new conditions, pivot when necessary, and embrace change as an opportunity for growth.

Leaders who embody resilience and adaptability are better equipped to guide their teams through turbulent times. They create a culture where challenges are seen as opportunities to learn and innovate rather than as insurmountable obstacles. This mindset not only helps the organization to survive in difficult times but also positions it to thrive in the long run.

The Mindset of a Resilient and Adaptable Leader

To lead with resilience and adaptability, you must first cultivate a mindset that embraces change, sees challenges as opportunities, and remains committed to growth, even in the face of uncertainty. This mindset allows you to navigate the inevitable ups and downs of leadership with grace and determination.

1. Embracing Challenges as Opportunities for Growth

Resilient leaders view challenges not as threats but as opportunities to learn, grow, and improve. They understand that every setback is a chance to develop new skills, gain new perspectives, and build a stronger, more resilient team.

Mindset: Adopt the belief that challenges are an integral part of growth. Understand that by facing and overcoming difficulties, you and your team can emerge stronger and more capable than before.

2. Staying Composed Under Pressure

Resilient leaders maintain their composure, even in the most stressful situations. They understand that their ability to stay calm and focused has a direct impact on their team's morale and performance.

Mindset: Cultivate a sense of inner calm and focus, especially during times of crisis. Recognize that your emotional state sets the tone for the entire team, and strive to be a steadying influence in turbulent times.

3. Being Open to Change and Adaptation

Adaptable leaders are not rigid in their thinking; they are open to new ideas, willing to pivot when necessary, and ready to embrace change. They understand that adaptability is crucial for staying competitive and relevant in a rapidly changing world.

Mindset: Embrace change as a constant in leadership. Understand that being adaptable is not a sign of weakness but a strength that allows you to navigate uncertainty and capitalize on new opportunities.

4. Fostering a Growth Mindset

A growth mindset is the belief that abilities and intelligence can be developed through hard work, learning, and perseverance. Resilient and adaptable leaders foster a growth mindset within themselves and their teams, encouraging continuous learning and improvement.

Mindset: Believe that you and your team can grow and improve through effort and experience. Encourage a culture of continuous learning, where challenges are viewed as opportunities to develop new skills and knowledge.

Behavioral Practices for Leading with Resilience and Adaptability

Once you have cultivated a resilient and adaptable mindset, the next step is to translate that mindset into behaviors that reinforce these qualities within your team. These behaviors are crucial for creating a culture where resilience and adaptability are the norm, not the exception.

1. Modeling Resilience in Action

Leaders set the example for how their teams respond to challenges. By demonstrating resilience in your own actions—whether by staying calm under pressure, bouncing back from setbacks, or maintaining a positive outlook—you inspire your team to do the same.

Behavioral Practices:

- **Stay calm in crisis:** In moments of crisis or stress, consciously focus on maintaining your composure. This doesn't mean suppressing your emotions but rather managing them in a way that helps you think clearly and act decisively by asking yourself: "What matters most at this moment, during this challenge? Where should I put my energy and focus instead of losing my temper?"

- **Show persistence:** When faced with obstacles, demonstrate persistence by continuing to work toward your goals despite setbacks, one step at a time. Share your experiences with your team to show that resilience involves effort and perseverance.

- **Practice optimism:** Cultivate a habit of finding the silver lining in difficult situations. Share positive perspectives with your team to help them stay motivated and focused on solutions rather than problems. When facing a problem or something goes wrong, don't focus on the limitations but on the possibilities (or even on the new opportunities given within this difficult situation) and the resources you have at your disposal to reach a solution.

By modeling resilience in your own behavior, you create a culture where your team feels empowered to face challenges head-on and bounce back from setbacks with renewed determination.

2. Encouraging Adaptability and Flexibility

Adaptable leaders encourage their teams to be flexible and open to change. They create an environment where experimentation is encouraged and where mistakes are seen as learning opportunities rather than failures.

Behavioral Practices:

- **Promote experimentation:** Encourage your team to try new approaches, even if there is a risk of failure. Support them in experimenting with different strategies and learning from the outcomes. When using a way of working for a long period of time, challenge it and question it by examining if there's another new and more effective way to do it.

- **Be open to feedback:** Show that you are open to feedback and willing to adjust your approach based on new information. This demonstrates that adaptability is a valued trait within the organization.

- **Embrace change:** When changes occur—whether due to external factors or internal decisions—embrace them with a positive attitude. Help your team see the potential benefits of the change and guide them through the transition. Instead of watching the wave of change going above you and take you away, ride it and go with it as a choice!

By encouraging adaptability and flexibility, you create a culture where your team feels confident in navigating change and where they are motivated to innovate and improve continuously.

3. Supporting Your Team Through Challenges

Resilient leaders provide support and guidance to their teams during challenging times. They recognize that resilience is not just an individual trait but a collective one, and they work to build resilience at the team level.

Behavioral Practices:

- **Provide emotional support:** Be attuned to the emotional needs of your team during difficult times. Offer empathy, encouragement, and reassurance to help them cope with stress and uncertainty. Ask them how they feel and what they think. Offer your help and guidance by asking them: "How can I support you?"

- **Facilitate problem-solving:** When challenges arise, work with your team to identify solutions. Encourage collaborative problem-solving and ensure that everyone has a role in overcoming obstacles.

- **Celebrate small wins:** Recognize and celebrate the small victories along the way. This helps to build momentum and keeps the team motivated, even when progress is slow.

By supporting your team through challenges, you help to build a culture of collective resilience, where everyone feels supported and empowered to overcome difficulties together.

4. Promoting Continuous Learning and Growth

Resilient and adaptable leaders understand that continuous learning is key to staying relevant and effective in a rapidly changing world. They promote a culture of learning within their teams, where every challenge is viewed as an opportunity to gain new skills and insights.

Behavioral Practices:

- **Encourage learning opportunities:** Provide your team with opportunities for training, development, and skill-building. Encourage them to take on new challenges that will help them grow.

- **Reflect on experiences:** After overcoming a challenge or navigating a change, take the time to reflect with your team on what was learned. Discuss what worked well, what didn't, and how the experience can inform future actions. Don't rush immediately to the next challenge or step, losing the precious opportunity for learning and growth, individually and as a team.

- **Foster a growth mindset:** Encourage your team to view challenges as opportunities to develop new skills and knowledge. Reinforce the belief that abilities can be developed through effort and experience. Train them to find at least one advantage and one opportunity a challenge carries within.

By promoting continuous learning and growth, you create a culture where resilience and adaptability are not just responses to challenges but proactive strategies for ongoing success.

Science-Based Insight

Recent research in neuroscience has shown that neuroplasticity plays a critical role in how the brain adapts to stress and change. Neuroplasticity refers to the brain's ability to reorganize itself by forming new neural connections in response to learning and experience. This ability underpins the cognitive flexibility and emotional regulation required for resilience and adaptability in dynamic environments (Brocardo et al., 2023).

Resilience, in particular, is supported by neural circuits in the prefrontal cortex (PFC) and the limbic system, which are crucial for managing emotional responses and stress. When leaders model resilience, they positively influence their team's ability to regulate stress, as the PFC helps to maintain control over emotional reactions, promoting a more stable and productive work environment (Lorsch et al., 2019; Brocardo et al., 2023).

Adaptability is closely linked to the brain's cognitive flexibility, governed by the PFC. Cognitive flexibility allows individuals to shift their thinking and adjust to new circumstances, which is essential in fast-changing organizational settings. Leaders who demonstrate and encourage adaptability stimulate these areas in their employees, enhancing creativity, innovation, and problem-solving skills (Kennedy, 2021).

By fostering resilience and adaptability, leaders can create a neurochemical environment that supports emotional well-being, cognitive flexibility, and continuous growth—all crucial elements for building a high-performing workplace culture.

Putting pen to paper

Exercise: The Resilience and Adaptability Action Plan

Objective: To develop and strengthen your resilience and adaptability as a leader by creating a personalized action plan that you can apply in your day-to-day leadership.

Instructions:

1. **Assess your current resilience and adaptability:** Begin by reflecting on your experiences with resilience and adaptability in your leadership role. Consider the following questions:

   - How do you typically respond to challenges or setbacks?

   - How well do you manage stress and maintain your composure under pressure?

   - How open are you to change, and how easily do you adapt to new circumstances?

- How do you support your team during times of change or crisis?

2. **Identify areas for growth:** Based on your self-assessment, identify specific areas where you could improve your resilience and adaptability. This might include better stress management, embracing change more readily, or providing stronger support to your team during challenging times.

3. **Set specific goals:** Set two or three specific goals that will help you build resilience and adaptability. These goals should be actionable, measurable, and aligned with the areas for growth you've identified. For example:

   - "I will practice mindfulness meditation for 10 minutes each day to improve my stress management and emotional regulation."

   - "I will seek feedback from my team after each major change initiative to learn how I can better support them in adapting to new circumstances."

   - "I will commit to viewing challenges as opportunities for growth by reflecting on the lessons learned from each setback."

4. **Develop strategies for achieving your goals:** For each goal, outline the specific strategies or actions you will take to achieve it. This might include adopting new practices, seeking out

resources, or making changes to your leadership approach. For example:

- For stress management: "I will schedule regular breaks throughout the day to practice deep breathing exercises and will attend a workshop on mindfulness techniques."

- For supporting your team: "I will hold weekly check-ins with my team during times of change to provide guidance, address concerns, and offer emotional support."

- For embracing change: "I will actively seek out opportunities to learn new skills or explore different perspectives, such as attending industry conferences or taking an online course."

5. **Implement and monitor your progress:** Begin implementing your action plan and monitor your progress over time. Keep a journal or log to track your experiences, challenges, and successes. Reflect on how your efforts are impacting your resilience, adaptability, and overall leadership effectiveness.

6. **Reflect and adjust:** After a few months, review your progress and reflect on what you've learned. Consider whether you've achieved your goals or if there are areas where you still need to

improve. Adjust your action plan as needed to continue building your resilience and adaptability.

By creating and following a resilience and adaptability action plan, you can strengthen these essential leadership qualities, enabling you to navigate challenges with confidence and lead your team through change with purpose and clarity.

Avoiding Leadership Pitfalls: The Risks of Rigidity and Burnout

While resilience and adaptability are crucial for effective leadership, it's important to recognize the pitfalls that can arise when these qualities are lacking. Leaders who are rigid in their thinking or who fail to manage stress effectively may inadvertently create a culture that is resistant to change, prone to burnout, and less capable of navigating challenges.

1. Rigidity and Resistance to Change

Leaders who are inflexible in their thinking or resistant to change may struggle to adapt to new conditions, leading to stagnation and missed opportunities. This rigidity can also create a culture where employees are hesitant to embrace change or to think creatively.

Consequences:

- **Decreased innovation:** A rigid approach to leadership stifles innovation, as employees are less likely to experiment or explore new ideas.

- **Lower adaptability:** Organizations led by rigid leaders may struggle to adapt to changes in the market or industry, leading to a loss of competitiveness.

- **Higher resistance to change:** Employees may become resistant to change if they perceive that their leaders are not open to new ideas or flexible in their approach.

2. Burnout and Decreased Resilience

Leaders who fail to manage stress effectively or who do not support their teams during challenging times may contribute to burnout and decreased resilience within the organization. Burnout can lead to lower productivity, higher turnover, and a negative impact on overall well-being.

Consequences:

- **Increased stress:** Poor stress management can lead to higher levels of stress and anxiety among employees, negatively impacting their mental and physical health.

- **Lower productivity:** Burnout reduces productivity, as employees struggle to maintain focus and motivation in the face of overwhelming stress.

- **Higher turnover:** Burnout can lead to higher turnover as employees seek out healthier work environments where they feel supported and valued.

3. Inadequate Support for Adaptation and Growth

Leaders who fail to provide adequate support for their teams during times of change may hinder their team's ability to adapt and grow. Without the right guidance and resources, employees may feel overwhelmed and ill-equipped to navigate new challenges.

Consequences:

- **Decreased learning and development:** A lack of support for learning and growth can limit employees' ability to develop new skills and knowledge, reducing their effectiveness in adapting to change.

- **Lower engagement:** Employees who feel unsupported during times of change may disengage from their work, leading to lower motivation and commitment.

- **Reduced resilience:** Inadequate support can weaken the overall resilience of the team, making it harder for the organization to recover from setbacks or to navigate ongoing challenges.

Conclusion: Resilience and Adaptability as Pillars of Leadership

Resilience and adaptability are not just skills; they are pillars that support effective leadership and organizational success. By leading with resilience, you demonstrate the ability to overcome challenges and maintain focus in the face of adversity. By fostering adaptability, you create a culture where change is embraced as an opportunity for growth, innovation, and continuous improvement.

In this chapter, we've explored how resilience and adaptability influence leadership and organizational culture. We've discussed the mindset necessary to cultivate these qualities, the behaviors that bring them to life, and the ripple effects they have on the organization as a whole. We've also examined the potential pitfalls of rigidity and burnout and the importance of maintaining flexibility, composure, and support in all interactions.

As you continue your leadership journey, remember that what you see is how you lead. By leading with resilience and adaptability, you not only strengthen your team but also lay the foundation for a high-performing, innovative, and resilient workplace culture.

In the chapters that follow, we will explore additional cognitive and behavioral practices that will help you refine your leadership approach and create a thriving, high-performing organizational culture. Together, we will uncover the full spectrum of leadership qualities that will empower you to lead with confidence, clarity, and resilience.

Practice Nr. 6: Accountability and Integrity

In leadership, accountability and integrity are not just desirable traits—they are essential. These qualities are the bedrock of trust and credibility, both within your team and with external stakeholders. Leaders who demonstrate accountability and integrity inspire confidence, foster a culture of responsibility, and set the standard for ethical behavior in their organizations.

In this chapter of *The Mirror Effect: What You See, Is How You Lead!*, we will explore the importance of accountability and integrity in leadership. We will examine the mindset required to embody these principles and the behaviors that reinforce them within your team. Additionally, we will delve into the neurological and psychological impact of accountability and integrity on employee trust, engagement, and overall organizational culture.

J. was the owner of a small but growing construction business. J. was known for his craftsmanship and dedication to his clients, and his hands-on approach earned him a strong reputation in the industry. However, as his business expanded, his approach to managing tasks began to create serious problems. J. had a habit of taking on too much himself, often assuring his team that he would handle certain tasks personally, only to find himself overwhelmed and unable to deliver on time. This lack of follow-through led to last-minute scrambles and put unnecessary pressure on his team.

J. prided himself on being involved in every project, but he struggled with delegating responsibilities. He often promised to complete key tasks—like securing permits, ordering materials, or meeting with clients—believing that his personal touch was essential. However, as his workload increased, he found it harder to keep up with these commitments. Rather than admitting that he needed help or that he couldn't meet the deadlines, he would delay communicating the status to his team until the situation had become urgent. This often led to rushed work, strained client relationships, and a stressed-out team.

One day, the company was working on a high-profile project that required meticulous planning and precise execution. J. had assured his team that he would take care of acquiring a crucial permit needed to start the construction. He had been confident that he could handle it, but as the project deadline approached, he realized he had forgotten to submit the necessary paperwork. By the time he acknowledged the mistake, the project was at a standstill, and the delay threatened to put the entire project behind schedule.

Frustrated and overwhelmed, J. called an emergency meeting with his team. The stress was palpable, and his employees were clearly upset. One of his foremen, Dave, spoke up, "J., this isn't the first time we've been left scrambling because something didn't get done in time. We're always in a rush because we don't know what's actually been handled until it's almost too late. We can't keep working like this."

J., feeling cornered, tried to defend himself. "I just wanted to make sure everything was done right. I didn't want to burden anyone else with it."

Dave shook his head. "But by not following through or letting us know in time, you're actually making things harder for all of us. We're your team—we're here to help, but we need to know what's really going on so we can do our jobs."

J. realized that his lack of accountability was eroding the trust and respect of his team. He reached out to me for advice, feeling both guilty and uncertain about how to move forward. During our conversation, I asked him, "J., why do you feel the need to handle so much on your own?"

He hesitated before admitting, "I've always felt that as the owner, it's my responsibility to oversee everything. I want things done right, and I guess I've been afraid that if I delegate too much, something might go wrong."

"But what's been the result of trying to do everything yourself?" I asked gently.

J. sighed. "I've been dropping the ball, and it's putting unnecessary stress on my team. They're frustrated with me, and I can see that it's affecting their work. I never meant to let them down, but I've been so focused on controlling everything that I've lost sight of the bigger picture."

"Accountability and integrity are about being honest with yourself and others," I explained. "It's not just about doing the work—it's about keeping your commitments and being transparent when you need help. Your team looks to you for leadership, and part of that is trusting them to handle their responsibilities while you focus on what you can realistically manage. How would things change if you started delegating tasks and communicating openly about what you can and can't do?"

J. nodded, understanding the importance of what I was saying. "I see that now. I've been holding onto too much, and it's causing more harm than good. I need to start trusting my team more and be upfront about what I can realistically handle."

The next day, J. called a meeting with his team, determined to make a change. "I owe you all an apology," he began. "I've been trying to do too much on my own, and it's led to last-minute problems that have put unnecessary pressure on all of you. That's not fair, and it's not how I want to lead this company. From now on, I'm going to be more upfront about what I can handle, and I'm going to start delegating tasks so we can work together more effectively."

He then outlined a plan to better distribute responsibilities, ensuring that tasks were clearly assigned and that deadlines were realistic. He also committed to regular check-ins to keep everyone informed about the status of ongoing projects.

Over the next few months, the atmosphere in the company began to improve. With tasks more evenly distributed, the team felt more in control and less stressed. Projects ran more smoothly, and client satisfaction improved. J.'s willingness to be accountable and delegate tasks restored trust within the team and reinforced a culture of integrity and collaboration.

Reflecting on the experience, J. realized that accountability and integrity were not just about personal responsibility—they were about leading by example and building trust within the team. By keeping his commitments, being honest about his limitations, and empowering his team, J. was able to turn things around and lead his company to greater success. He learned that true leadership involves not only doing the right thing but also being transparent and dependable, ensuring that everyone on the team can perform at their best.

Understanding Accountability and Integrity in Leadership

Accountability in leadership means taking responsibility for your actions, decisions, and their outcomes—whether they are successes or failures. It involves being transparent about your role in situations, owning up to mistakes, and following through on commitments. Integrity, on the other hand, is the quality of being honest, ethical, and consistent in your actions, regardless of external pressures or potential consequences.

When leaders prioritize accountability and integrity, they create a culture of trust and excellence. Employees are more likely to respect leaders who hold themselves accountable and who consistently act with integrity. This trust forms the foundation for strong, effective teams that are committed to high standards and ethical behavior.

The Mindset of an Accountable and Integrity-Driven Leader

To lead with accountability and integrity, you must first cultivate a mindset that values responsibility, honesty, and ethical behavior. This mindset is not just about adhering to rules or avoiding mistakes—it's about consistently doing what is right and setting a positive example for others to follow.

1. Taking Ownership of Your Actions

Accountable leaders understand that they are responsible for their actions, decisions, and their impact on others. They do not shy away from admitting mistakes or shortcomings; instead, they take ownership of them and work to make things right.

Mindset: Embrace the belief that true leadership involves taking full responsibility for your actions. Recognize that by owning your mistakes as well as your successes, you build credibility and trust with your team.

2. Committing to Ethical Behavior

Leaders with integrity are committed to doing what is right, even when it is difficult or when no one is watching. They understand that ethical behavior is not just about following the rules but about adhering to a moral compass that guides their decisions and actions.

Mindset: Develop a strong commitment to ethical behavior. Understand that integrity is the cornerstone of trust and that your actions should consistently reflect your values and principles.

3. Leading by Example

Accountable and integrity-driven leaders lead by example, demonstrating the behaviors and values they expect from their team. They understand that their actions speak louder than words and that their team will follow the example they set.

Mindset: Believe that your behavior sets the standard for your team. Commit to modeling the accountability and integrity you expect from others, knowing that your actions will influence the culture of the entire organization.

4. Valuing Transparency and Honesty

Leaders who value accountability and integrity prioritize transparency and honesty in their communication. They understand that being open about their decisions and actions builds trust and fosters a culture of honesty and openness within the team.

Mindset: Cultivate a mindset that values transparency and honesty. Recognize that being forthright about your decisions, intentions, and mistakes not only builds trust but also encourages others to do the same.

Behavioral Practices for Leading with Accountability and Integrity

Once you have cultivated an accountable and integrity-driven mindset, the next step is to translate that mindset into behaviors that reinforce these principles within your team. These behaviors are crucial for creating a culture where accountability and integrity are the norm, not the exception.

1. Owning Your Decisions and Outcomes

Accountable leaders do not deflect blame or make excuses when things go wrong. Instead, they take responsibility for their decisions and the outcomes that result from them, whether positive or negative.

Behavioral Practices:

- **Admit mistakes:** When you make a mistake, acknowledge it openly and take responsibility for the consequences. Avoid shifting blame to others or external factors.

- **Provide solutions:** After acknowledging a mistake, focus on finding solutions. Work with your team to address the issue and prevent similar mistakes in the future.

- **Follow through on commitments:** Ensure that you follow through on the commitments you make. If circumstances change, communicate clearly and take responsibility for any adjustments needed.

By owning your decisions and outcomes, you demonstrate accountability in action, setting a powerful example for your team and fostering a culture of responsibility and trust.

2. Demonstrating Ethical Decision-Making

Leaders with integrity consistently make ethical decisions, even when it is difficult or when there may be pressure to do otherwise. They consider the long-term impact of their actions on their team, organization, and stakeholders.

Behavioral Practices:

- **Consider the impact:** Before making a decision, consider its ethical implications and how it will affect others. Make choices that align with your values and the organization's principles.

- **Be consistent:** Ensure that your actions are consistent with your words and values. Avoid making exceptions or compromises that could undermine your integrity.

- **Stand by your principles:** In situations where you face pressure to act unethically, stand by your principles. Be willing to make difficult decisions that prioritize doing what is right over what is expedient.

By demonstrating ethical decision-making, you reinforce the importance of integrity within your team and create a culture where ethical behavior is expected and valued.

3. Encouraging Accountability in Others

Accountable leaders not only hold themselves responsible but also encourage accountability within their teams. They set clear expectations, provide feedback, and ensure that everyone understands their role in achieving team goals.

Behavioral Practices:

- **Set clear expectations:** Communicate your expectations for accountability clearly and consistently. Ensure that everyone on your team understands their responsibilities and what is expected of them.

- **Provide constructive feedback:** When team members fall short of expectations, provide constructive feedback that focuses on improvement rather than punishment. Encourage them to take ownership of their actions and learn from their experiences.

- **Recognize accountability:** When team members demonstrate accountability, recognize and reward their behavior. This reinforces the importance of accountability and motivates others to follow suit.

By encouraging accountability in others, you create a culture where everyone takes responsibility for their actions, leading to higher performance, greater trust, and stronger team cohesion.

4. Building Trust Through Transparency and Integrity

Transparency and integrity are key to building trust within your team. Leaders who are open about their decisions, honest in their communication, and consistent in their actions create an environment where trust can flourish.

Behavioral Practices:

- **Be transparent:** Share information openly with your team, including the rationale behind your decisions and any challenges or uncertainties you are facing. This builds trust and keeps everyone informed.

- **Communicate honestly:** Always communicate honestly, even when the truth is difficult. Avoid sugarcoating or withholding information, as this can erode trust.

- **Act consistently:** Ensure that your actions align with your words and values. Consistency in behavior builds credibility and reinforces your integrity.

By building trust through transparency and integrity, you create a culture where team members feel confident in their leaders and in each other, leading to greater collaboration, engagement, and overall success.

Science-based Insight

Accountability and integrity are closely linked to the brain's reward and social bonding systems. These qualities are fundamental to building trust, which is essential for effective teamwork and collaboration. The brain's prefrontal cortex, responsible for decision-making and social behavior, plays a key role in how we perceive and respond to accountability and integrity in others.

According to Stanford (2017), when leaders demonstrate accountability and integrity, it activates the brain's oxytocin system, often referred to as the "trust hormone." Oxytocin is associated with feelings of trust, bonding, and social connection. When employees perceive their leaders as accountable and trustworthy, their brains release oxytocin, which enhances their sense of connection, loyalty, and commitment to the organization.

Moreover, the brain's reward system, which includes the release of dopamine, is activated when individuals engage in ethical behavior and make decisions that align with their values. This neurochemical response reinforces positive behavior, creating a cycle where accountability and integrity lead to greater satisfaction, motivation, and overall well-being.

By fostering accountability and integrity, leaders can create a neurochemical environment that supports trust, ethical behavior, and strong social bonds, all of which are critical for building a high-performing workplace culture.

Putting pen to paper

Exercise: The Accountability and Integrity Self-Assessment

Objective: To assess your current level of accountability and integrity as a leader and to develop strategies for strengthening these qualities in your leadership approach.

Instructions:

1. **Conduct a self-assessment:** Begin by reflecting on your experiences with accountability and integrity in your leadership role. Consider the following questions:

   - How do you typically respond when you make a mistake or face a setback?

   - How consistent are your actions with your words and values?

- How transparent and honest are you in your communication with your team?

- How do you encourage accountability and integrity within your team?

2. **Identify strengths and areas for improvement:** Based on your self-assessment, identify specific areas where you excel in accountability and integrity, as well as areas where you could improve. This might include being more transparent in your communication, taking greater ownership of your decisions, or modeling ethical behavior more consistently.

3. **Set specific goals:** Set two or three specific goals that will help you strengthen your accountability and integrity as a leader. These goals should be actionable, measurable, and aligned with the areas for improvement you've identified. For example:

   - "I will take full ownership of any mistakes I make and communicate openly with my team about how I plan to address them."

   - "I will ensure that my actions are consistent with my values and the organization's principles, even in difficult situations."

   - "I will prioritize transparency in all my communications, sharing both successes and challenges with my team."

4. **Develop strategies for achieving your goals:** For each goal, outline the specific strategies or actions you will take to achieve

it. This might include adopting new practices, seeking out resources, or making changes to your leadership approach. For example:

- For transparency: "I will schedule regular team meetings to discuss ongoing projects, challenges, and decisions, ensuring that everyone is informed and has the opportunity to ask questions."

- For ethical behavior: "I will create a personal code of ethics to guide my decision-making and will regularly review it to ensure I am staying true to my values."

- For encouraging accountability: "I will establish clear expectations for accountability within my team and will provide regular feedback to help team members take ownership of their actions."

5. **Implement and monitor your progress:** Begin implementing your action plan and monitor your progress over time. Keep a journal or log to track your experiences, challenges, and successes. Reflect on how your efforts are impacting your accountability, integrity, and overall leadership effectiveness.

6. **Reflect and adjust:** After a few months, review your progress and reflect on what you've learned. Consider whether you've achieved your goals or if there are areas where you still need to improve. Adjust your action plan as needed to continue strengthening your accountability and integrity.

By creating and following an accountability and integrity self-assessment, you can reinforce these essential leadership qualities, enabling you to build trust, inspire confidence, and lead your team with unwavering ethical standards.

Avoiding Leadership Pitfalls: The Dangers of Blame and Dishonesty

While accountability and integrity are essential for effective leadership, it's important to recognize the pitfalls that can arise when these qualities are lacking. Leaders who avoid accountability or who act dishonestly can create a culture of blame, mistrust, and unethical behavior.

1. Blame Shifting and Avoidance of Responsibility

Leaders who avoid taking responsibility for their actions or who shift blame onto others can create a toxic culture where accountability is absent. This can lead to a lack of trust, poor team dynamics, and lower overall performance.

Consequences:

- **Decreased morale:** When leaders shift blame or avoid responsibility, it undermines morale and trust within the team. Employees may feel unsupported and demotivated.

- **Lower accountability:** A lack of accountability at the leadership level can lead to a culture where no one takes responsibility for their actions, resulting in lower performance and poor outcomes.

- **Increased conflict:** Blame-shifting can lead to increased conflict within the team, as individuals seek to protect themselves rather than collaborate effectively.

2. Dishonesty and Erosion of Trust

Leaders who act dishonestly or who fail to be transparent in their communication risk eroding trust within the organization. Dishonesty can lead to a breakdown in relationships, decreased engagement, and a negative impact on the organization's reputation.

Consequences:

- **Loss of trust:** Dishonesty erodes trust between leaders and employees, leading to a breakdown in communication and collaboration.

- **Reduced engagement:** Employees are less likely to be engaged and motivated when they perceive that their leaders are not being honest or transparent.

- **Reputational damage:** Dishonesty can lead to reputational damage for the organization, making it harder to attract and retain top talent and customers.

3. Inconsistent Behavior and Ethical Compromises

Leaders who act inconsistently or who compromise their ethical standards for short-term gain can undermine the integrity of the organization. This can lead to a culture where unethical behavior is tolerated or even encouraged.

Consequences:

- **Decreased credibility:** Inconsistent behavior and ethical compromises can damage a leader's credibility, making it harder to inspire trust and loyalty.

- **Increased risk:** Unethical behavior increases the risk of legal, financial, and reputational damage, which can have long-term consequences for the organization.

- **Negative workplace culture:** A culture where ethical standards are compromised can lead to a toxic work environment where trust is low and unethical behavior is common.

Conclusion: Accountability and Integrity as Pillars of Leadership

Accountability and integrity are not just about following rules or avoiding mistakes—they are about taking ownership, doing what is right, and setting the standard for ethical behavior in your organization. By leading with accountability, you demonstrate responsibility and build trust. By leading with integrity, you create a culture where honesty, transparency, and ethical behavior are valued and expected.

In this chapter, we've explored how accountability and integrity influence leadership and organizational culture. We've discussed the mindset necessary to embody these principles, the behaviors that bring them to life, and the ripple effects they have on the organization as a whole. We've also examined the potential pitfalls of blame and dishonesty and the importance of maintaining consistency, transparency, and ethical standards in all interactions.

As you continue your leadership journey, remember that what you see is how you lead. By leading with accountability and integrity, you not only strengthen your team but also lay the foundation for a high-performing, trustworthy, and ethical workplace culture.

In the chapters that follow, we will explore additional cognitive and behavioral practices that will help you refine your leadership approach and create a thriving, high-performing organizational culture. Together, we will uncover the full spectrum of leadership qualities that will empower you to lead with confidence, clarity, and integrity.

Practice Nr. 7: Empowerment and Trust

Empowerment and trust are critical components of effective leadership. Leaders who empower their team members to make decisions, take ownership, and contribute their unique talents create an environment where individuals feel valued, motivated, and capable of achieving great things. Trust, in turn, is the foundation that allows empowerment to flourish. When leaders trust their teams, they build a culture of confidence, accountability, and mutual respect.

In this chapter of *The Mirror Effect: What You See, Is How You Lead!*, we will explore the importance of empowerment and trust in leadership. We will examine the mindset required to truly empower others and the behaviors that build and maintain trust within your team. Additionally, we will delve into the neurological and psychological impact of empowerment and trust on employee engagement, performance, and overall organizational success.

A. was the manager of a regional sales team for a telecommunications company. A. was deeply committed to his team's success and had high expectations for their performance. He believed in pushing his team hard to achieve their targets, and he was always quick to point out when someone made a mistake or failed to meet expectations. However, in his zeal to drive results, A. developed a habit of focusing almost exclusively on his team members' faults and weaknesses, often overlooking their strengths and achievements.

During team meetings, A. would review sales reports and immediately zero in on the areas where numbers fell short. "T., you missed your quota again this month. What's going on?" he would ask, with a tone that left little room for explanation. "S., you've been making too many errors in your client presentations. You need to tighten up your approach." These critiques were delivered without much acknowledgment of the hard work and successes his team members had achieved. Over time, the team began to feel demoralized and undervalued, and their performance started to decline.

The situation came to a head when a particularly important deal fell through. A. was furious and called an emergency meeting to address the issue. Once again, he focused on what had gone wrong, pointing out the mistakes that had been made without recognizing the effort the team had put in. The atmosphere in the room was tense; the team members looked defeated, and it was clear that morale was at an all-time low.

After the meeting, one of his senior salespeople, M., approached A. privately. "A.," she began cautiously, "I know you want us to improve, but constantly hearing only about our faults is really wearing us down. We're trying our best, but it feels like nothing we do is ever good enough."

A. was taken aback. He had never intended to demoralize his team—he thought that by pointing out their weaknesses, he was helping them to grow and improve. But M.'s words made him realize that his approach was having the opposite effect.

Concerned and wanting to make things right, A. reached out to me for advice. During our conversation, I asked him, "A., how often do you recognize your team's strengths and accomplishments?"

He paused, reflecting on his recent interactions. "I guess I haven't done that much. I've been so focused on what needs fixing that I haven't really acknowledged what they're doing well."

"Empowerment and trust are essential for any team to thrive," I explained. "When you only focus on what's wrong, you're not giving your team the confidence they need to excel. By consistently pointing out their faults without recognizing their strengths, you're eroding their trust in themselves and in you as a leader. What if, instead of just highlighting their weaknesses, you started to empower them by acknowledging their achievements and trusting them to learn from their mistakes?"

A. nodded slowly, beginning to see the impact of his actions. "I didn't realize how much that could affect them. But how do I start changing that now?"

"Start by shifting your focus," I suggested. "Make it a point to recognize the strengths and successes of your team members. When mistakes happen, address them constructively but also highlight what they're doing well. Show them that you trust them to grow and improve, and empower them by giving them more autonomy to take ownership of their work."

Determined to make a change, A. called another meeting with his team. This time, he approached it differently. "I want to start by acknowledging the hard work you've all been putting in," he began. "T., I noticed that you've been really proactive in reaching out to new clients, and that's making a difference. S., your latest presentation was solid—you really connected with the client, and that's what we need more of."

The team was surprised by this new approach, but they appreciated the recognition. A. then addressed the areas that needed improvement, but he did so with a more supportive tone. "I know we've had some setbacks, but I trust that we can turn things around. Let's work together to figure out what we can do better, and I'm confident we'll get back on track."

Over the next few weeks, A. made a concerted effort to balance his feedback, ensuring that he recognized his team's successes as well as addressing their challenges. He also started to delegate more responsibility, giving his team members the autonomy to manage their own clients and make decisions. As a result, the team's morale began to improve, and they started to regain their confidence. Performance gradually picked up, and the atmosphere in the office became more positive and collaborative.

Reflecting on the experience, A. realized that empowerment and trust were not just about giving orders or pointing out mistakes—they were about building a team's confidence and creating an environment where people felt valued and capable. By focusing on his team's strengths and showing them that he trusted them to succeed, A. was able to foster a culture of mutual respect and high performance. He learned that true leadership involves not just correcting mistakes but also empowering others to achieve their best by recognizing their potential and trusting them to grow.

The Mindset of a Leader Who Values Empowerment and Trust

To lead with empowerment and trust, you must first adopt a mindset that values the contributions of others and believes in their potential. This mindset involves letting go of the need to control every detail and instead focusing on enabling your team to succeed.

1. Believing in the Potential of Others

Leaders who empower their teams believe in the potential of each individual to contribute meaningfully. They recognize that every team member brings unique strengths and perspectives that can drive the organization forward.

Mindset: Embrace the belief that your team members are capable and talented individuals who can make valuable contributions. Trust in their abilities and encourage them to take ownership of their work.

2. Letting Go of Control

Empowerment requires leaders to let go of the need to control every aspect of their team's work. This doesn't mean abandoning oversight but rather trusting your team to make decisions and manage their responsibilities effectively.

Mindset: Develop a mindset that prioritizes outcomes over control. Understand that by giving your team the autonomy to make decisions, you enable them to grow, innovate, and take ownership of their success.

3. Fostering a Culture of Accountability

Empowered teams are also accountable teams. Leaders who value empowerment and trust ensure that responsibilities are clear and that team members are held accountable for their actions and results.

Mindset: Cultivate a mindset that values accountability as a natural extension of empowerment. Encourage your team to take responsibility for their work, knowing that they are trusted to deliver results.

4. Building and Maintaining Trust

Trust is the foundation of empowerment. Leaders who prioritize trust work to build and maintain it through consistent actions, open communication, and integrity.

Mindset: Believe that trust is earned through consistent, honest, and transparent behavior. Commit to building and maintaining trust with your team by demonstrating integrity and reliability in all your interactions.

Behavioral Practices for Leading with Empowerment and Trust

Once you have cultivated a mindset that values empowerment and trust, the next step is to translate that mindset into behaviors that reinforce these principles within your team. These behaviors are crucial for creating a culture where empowerment and trust are consistently practiced and deeply ingrained.

1. Delegating Responsibility and Authority

Leaders who empower their teams delegate not just tasks but also responsibility and authority. They trust their team members to make decisions and take ownership of their work.

Behavioral Practices:

- **Delegate decisions:** Assign decision-making authority to your team members, especially in areas where they have expertise. Allow them to make key decisions without micromanagement.

- **Set clear expectations:** When delegating responsibility, ensure that expectations are clear, and that team members understand the goals, boundaries, and resources available to them.

- **Provide support:** While delegating authority, offer support and guidance as needed. Be available to answer questions or provide feedback, but resist the urge to take over or micromanage.

By delegating responsibility and authority, you demonstrate trust in your team's abilities and encourage them to take ownership of their work.

2. Encouraging Initiative and Innovation

Empowered teams are more likely to take initiative and explore innovative ideas. Leaders who value empowerment create an environment where team members feel safe to experiment, take risks, and learn from their experiences.

Behavioral Practices:

- **Encourage risk-taking:** Create a safe environment where team members feel comfortable taking risks and trying new approaches. Emphasize that mistakes are opportunities for learning and growth.

- **Reward Innovation:** Recognize and reward innovative ideas and initiatives, even if they don't always lead to immediate success. Celebrate creativity and encourage continuous improvement.

- **Foster a growth mindset:** Encourage your team to adopt a growth mindset, where challenges are seen as opportunities to develop new skills and knowledge.

By encouraging initiative and innovation, you empower your team to explore new possibilities and drive the organization forward.

3. Building Trust Through Transparency and Communication

Trust is built on open communication and transparency. Leaders who prioritize trust ensure that their actions and decisions are transparent and that they communicate openly with their team.

Behavioral Practices:

- **Be transparent:** Share information openly with your team, including the rationale behind decisions, challenges, and changes. Transparency builds trust and keeps everyone aligned.

- **Communicate regularly:** Maintain regular communication with your team, providing updates, feedback, and opportunities for dialogue. Open communication fosters trust and ensures that everyone feels informed and connected.

- **Act consistently:** Ensure that your actions are consistent with your words. Consistency in behavior builds credibility and reinforces trust within the team.

By building trust through transparency and communication, you create a strong foundation for empowerment and collective success.

4. Recognizing and Celebrating Successes

Empowerment is reinforced when leaders recognize and celebrate the successes of their team members. Acknowledging individual and team achievements fosters a sense of pride and motivation.

Behavioral Practices:

- **Celebrate achievements:** Recognize and celebrate both individual and team successes. Publicly acknowledge contributions and highlight how they align with the organization's goals.

- **Provide positive feedback:** Offer positive feedback regularly, focusing on the specific actions and behaviors that led to success. Positive reinforcement strengthens trust and encourages continued high performance.

- **Encourage peer recognition:** Promote a culture where team members recognize and celebrate each other's successes. Peer recognition enhances teamwork and reinforces a collaborative spirit.

By recognizing and celebrating successes, you reinforce the value of empowerment and trust, motivating your team to continue striving for excellence.

Science-based Insight

Neuroscience research emphasizes how these leadership qualities activate key systems in the brain that enhance motivation and social connection. Dopamine, often called the "reward" neurotransmitter, plays a critical role when individuals feel empowered and trusted. The release of dopamine boosts motivation, job satisfaction, and overall well-being as employees gain ownership of their work (Kennedy, 2021).

Additionally, oxytocin, known as the "bonding hormone," is crucial for establishing trust. When leaders show trust in their employees, it triggers the release of oxytocin, which fosters social bonding and strengthens the relationship between the leader and the team. This neurochemical response contributes to higher levels of engagement, collaboration, and loyalty within the team (Zak, 2017; Kennedy, 2021).

By promoting a culture of empowerment and trust, leaders can create a neurochemical environment that enhances productivity, satisfaction, and emotional connection, ultimately leading to a high-performing workplace culture.

Putting pen to paper

Exercise: The Empowerment and Trust Action Plan

Objective: To create a structured action plan that will help you develop and strengthen empowerment and trust within your leadership approach, fostering a culture where these principles are consistently reinforced.

Instructions:

1. **Assess your current empowerment and trust practices:** Begin by reflecting on how you currently empower and trust your team members. Consider the following questions:

   - How often do you delegate responsibility and authority to your team members?

   - How much autonomy do you give your team to make decisions and manage their work?

   - How do you demonstrate trust in your team's abilities and judgment?

   - How do you encourage initiative and recognize success within your team?

2. **Identify areas for improvement:** Based on your self-assessment, identify specific areas where you can enhance your empowerment and trust practices. This might include delegating more responsibilities, improving transparency, or fostering a more open and collaborative environment.

3. **Set specific goals:** Set two or three specific goals that will help you strengthen empowerment and trust within your team. These goals should be actionabl measurable, and aligned with the areas for improvement you've identified. For example:

   - "I will delegate key decision-making responsibilities to my team members for the next major project."

   - "I will conduct regular one-on-one meetings to discuss my team's progress and offer support without micromanaging."

   - "I will actively recognize and celebrate team members who take initiative and demonstrate ownership of their work."

4. **Develop an empowerment and trust strategy:** Create a strategy that outlines how you will implement your goals. This strategy should include regular time slots for delegating tasks, offering support, and recognizing achievements. For example:

   - "I will identify specific tasks and decisions to delegate during our weekly team meetings."

   - "I will provide constructive feedback and support during our one-on-one meetings, ensuring that I offer guidance without taking over."

   - "I will publicly acknowledge and reward team members who demonstrate initiative and deliver exceptional results."

5. **Foster a culture of empowerment and trust:** Encourage your team to adopt a collaborative mindset by promoting open communication, shared accountability, and mutual respect. Create opportunities for team members to work together and to support each other in achieving common goals.

6. **Monitor and adjust your plan:** Regularly review your empowerment and trust action plan to assess its effectiveness. Seek feedback from your team on how these practices are impacting them and make adjustments as needed to ensure they remain meaningful and impactful.

By creating and following an empowerment and trust action plan, you can ensure that these principles are consistently reinforced, leading to higher levels of motivation, engagement, and collective success within your team. This commitment to empowering and trusting your team not only benefits them but also strengthens your leadership and contributes to a positive and high-performing workplace culture.

Avoiding Leadership Pitfalls:
The Dangers of Micromanagement and Distrust

While empowerment and trust are essential for effective leadership, it's important to recognize the pitfalls that can arise when these principles are neglected. Leaders who fail to empower their teams or who foster an environment of distrust may create a culture of micromanagement, disengagement, and low morale.

1. Micromanagement and Loss of Autonomy

Leaders who micromanage their teams undermine empowerment by taking control over every decision and detail. This can lead to a loss of autonomy, reduced creativity, and disengagement among team members.

Consequences:

- **Decreased motivation:** Micromanagement erodes motivation, as employees may feel that their contributions are undervalued or unnecessary.

- **Lower innovation:** A lack of autonomy stifles innovation, as employees are less likely to take risks or propose new ideas.

- **Higher stress:** Micromanagement increases stress levels, as employees may feel constantly scrutinized and pressured to conform to rigid expectations.

2. Distrust and Erosion of Confidence

Leaders who do not trust their teams may create an environment of distrust and low morale. Without trust, employees may feel demoralized, unsupported, and less committed to their work.

Consequences:

- **Decreased engagement:** A lack of trust leads to disengagement, as employees may feel disconnected from their work and the organization's goals.

- **Lower productivity:** Distrust undermines productivity, as employees may be less motivated to put in their best effort or to take initiative.

- **Increased turnover:** Employees who feel distrusted are more likely to leave the organization in search of a workplace where they feel valued and trusted.

3. Reduced Accountability and Ownership

Leaders who fail to empower their teams may struggle with fostering accountability and ownership. Without empowerment, employees may feel less responsible for their work and less motivated to achieve high standards.

Consequences:

- **Lower performance:** A lack of accountability leads to lower performance, as employees may not feel responsible for meeting their goals or delivering quality results.

- **Reduced initiative:** Without ownership, employees may be less likely to take initiative or to go above and beyond in their work.

- **Weaker team dynamics:** A lack of empowerment can weaken team dynamics, as employees may feel disconnected from their responsibilities and from each other.

Conclusion: Empowerment and Trust as Pillars of Leadership

Empowerment and trust are not just leadership strategies; they are the pillars that support innovation, engagement, and collective success. By leading with empowerment, you give your team the autonomy and authority to take ownership of their work, unlocking their full potential. By leading with trust, you create a culture of confidence, accountability, and mutual respect where everyone feels valued and motivated to contribute their best.

In this chapter, we've explored how empowerment and trust influence leadership and organizational culture. We've discussed the mindset necessary to empower others, the behaviors that build and maintain trust, and the ripple effects that empowerment and trust have on the organization as a whole. We've also examined the potential pitfalls of micromanagement and distrust and the importance of maintaining a commitment to these principles in all aspects of leadership.

As you continue your leadership journey, remember that what you see is how you lead. By leading with empowerment and trust, you not only strengthen your team but also lay the foundation for a high-performing, innovative, and engaged workplace culture.

In the chapters that follow, we will explore additional cognitive and behavioral practices that will help you refine your leadership approach and create a thriving, high-performing organizational culture.

Together, we will uncover the full spectrum of leadership qualities that will empower you to lead with confidence, clarity, and a commitment to empowering others.

Practice Nr. 8: Commitment to Continuous Learning

In the rapidly evolving landscape of modern organizations, the ability to learn and adapt is more critical than ever. Leaders who commit to continuous learning not only enhance their own skills and knowledge but also foster a culture of growth and innovation within their teams. This commitment to learning fuels personal and organizational development, driving success in an increasingly complex and competitive environment.

In this chapter of *The Mirror Effect: What You See, Is How You Lead!*, we will explore the importance of continuous learning in leadership. We will examine the mindset required to embrace lifelong learning and the behaviors that support and promote learning within your team. Additionally, we will delve into the neurological and psychological impact of continuous learning on creativity, adaptability, and overall organizational success.

R., the CEO of a mid-sized manufacturing company, had experienced steady growth over the years. R. was proud of the company's success and had built a solid reputation in the industry. However, as the market began to shift and competition intensified, R. recognized the need to bring in fresh perspectives to keep the company competitive. He decided to hire experienced executives from outside the company—leaders with a track record of innovation and a deep understanding of new industry trends.

R. hired these executives with the hope that they would bring new ideas and strategies to the table. He wanted them to lead their departments with fresh approaches and to introduce the latest industry best practices. However, despite his initial intentions, R. struggled to let go of the company's traditional ways of doing things. Whenever the new executives proposed changes, R. would push back, insisting that they stick to the methods that had worked in the past. He often said, "We've always done it this way, and it's what made us successful. Why fix what isn't broken?"

This resistance to change began to frustrate the new executives. They had been brought in to innovate and lead, but they found themselves stifled by R.'s insistence on maintaining the status quo. As a result, the company began to miss out on opportunities to modernize and adapt to the changing market. Sales began to stagnate, and the once-enthusiastic executives started to feel demoralized, questioning why they had been hired if their expertise wasn't being valued.

One day, during a leadership meeting, the new Head of Marketing, L., presented a plan to overhaul the company's branding strategy. She proposed leveraging up-to-date marketing tools and data analytics to better target emerging customer segments—a strategy that had proven successful in her previous roles. However, R. immediately shot down the idea. "Our brand has always been about tradition," he said firmly. "I don't see why we need to change what's been working for years."

After the meeting, L. asked to speak with R. privately. "R.," she began cautiously, "I was brought in to help the company grow and adapt to new challenges. But every time I suggest a new approach, it feels like you're not open to it. I understand that the old ways have worked in the past, but the market is changing, and if we don't evolve, we risk falling behind."

R. was taken aback by L.'s candid feedback. He had always believed in the importance of learning from others, but he realized that his actions weren't aligning with that belief. He reached out to me for advice, concerned that his resistance to change was holding the company back. During our conversation, I asked him, "R., why did you hire these new executives?"

He thought for a moment before replying, "I wanted fresh ideas and new strategies to help the company grow. I know the industry is changing, and I thought bringing in people with different experiences would give us an edge."

"And how has that been working out so far?" I asked gently.

R. sighed. "Not well. I keep pushing back on their ideas because I'm afraid of losing what made us successful in the first place. But now, I'm worried that we're not moving forward at all."

"Commitment to continuous learning means being open to new ideas and willing to adapt, even when it challenges your comfort zone," I explained. "By hiring these executives, you've already recognized the need for change. But true growth happens when you're willing to let go of old practices and embrace new ways of thinking. How do you think the company would benefit if you started trusting your new leaders and their expertise?"

R. nodded slowly, beginning to see the impact of his actions. "I hired them because I believed they could help us grow, but I haven't given them the chance to do that. I need to start listening and learning from them, just as I expect my team to learn from me."

Determined to change his approach, R. called another meeting with his leadership team. This time, he spoke with humility and openness. "I've realized that I've been holding us back by not fully embracing the new ideas and strategies you've brought to the table," he admitted. "I hired each of you because I trust your expertise and believe that you can help take this company to the next level. Moving forward, I want us to work together to integrate these new approaches, and I'm committed to learning alongside you."

The executives were relieved and encouraged by R.'s change in attitude. With his support, they began to implement the new strategies they had been proposing. L.'s marketing plan overhaul was rolled out, and it quickly started to show results, attracting also a younger customer base. Other departments also began to modernize their processes, incorporating the latest technologies and best practices that the new executives had been eager to introduce.

As the company started to evolve, R. noticed a renewed sense of energy and innovation within the team. The sales figures began to improve, and the company regained its competitive edge in the market. More importantly, R. himself felt re-energized, realizing that his willingness to learn and adapt had not only benefited the company but had also reignited his passion for leadership.

Reflecting on the experience, R. learned that commitment to continuous learning wasn't just about bringing in new ideas—it was about being willing to challenge old beliefs and embrace change. By trusting his team and being open to new ways of thinking, he was able to lead the company through a period of growth and transformation. R. understood that true leadership requires not only the ability to teach but also the humility to learn, ensuring that the organization can continue to grow and thrive in an ever-changing world.

Understanding Continuous Learning in Leadership

Continuous learning in leadership is the ongoing process of acquiring new knowledge, skills, and insights. It involves a proactive approach to personal and professional development, as well as a commitment to fostering a learning culture within the organization. Leaders who prioritize continuous learning are better equipped to navigate changes, solve complex problems, and inspire innovation within their teams.

A commitment to continuous learning is not just about attending workshops or earning certifications; it's about cultivating a mindset of curiosity, openness, and growth. It's about recognizing that learning is a lifelong journey, one that enhances not only your own leadership capabilities but also the collective potential of your team.

The Mindset of a Leader
Committed to Continuous Learning

To lead with a commitment to continuous learning, you must first adopt a mindset that values curiosity, growth, and the pursuit of knowledge. This mindset involves embracing the idea that learning never stops and that every experience offers an opportunity to gain new insights and skills.

1. Cultivating Curiosity and Openness

Leaders who are committed to continuous learning are naturally curious. They have a genuine interest in exploring new ideas, perspectives, and ways of doing things. This curiosity drives them to seek out new knowledge and to remain open to learning from every situation.

Mindset: Embrace the belief that there is always more to learn. Recognize that curiosity is the engine of growth and that by staying open to new experiences and ideas, you expand your understanding and capabilities.

2. Embracing a Growth Mindset

A growth mindset is the belief that abilities and intelligence can be developed through effort, learning, and perseverance. Leaders with a growth mindset see challenges as opportunities to learn and improve rather than as obstacles to be avoided.

Mindset: Develop a growth mindset by viewing challenges as opportunities for learning and growth. Understand that your abilities are not fixed but can be enhanced through continuous effort and experience.

3. Valuing Lifelong Learning

Leaders who are committed to continuous learning see learning as a lifelong journey, not a destination. They recognize that there is always room for improvement and that staying ahead in today's world requires ongoing development.

Mindset: Value the process of learning as a lifelong endeavor. Commit to regularly seeking out new knowledge, skills, and experiences that will enhance your leadership and contribute to your personal and professional growth.

4. Encouraging Learning in Others

Leaders committed to continuous learning not only focus on their own development but also encourage and support the learning of others. They understand that a learning culture benefits the entire organization, leading to greater innovation, adaptability, and success.

Mindset: Believe in the power of collective learning. Encourage and support your team in their own learning journeys, recognizing that their growth contributes to the overall success of the organization.

Behavioral Practices for Leading with a Commitment to Continuous Learning

Once you have cultivated a mindset that values continuous learning, the next step is to translate that mindset into behaviors that promote and support learning within your team. These behaviors are crucial for creating a culture where continuous learning is prioritized and valued.

1. Leading by Example

Leaders who are committed to continuous learning lead by example. They demonstrate their commitment to learning by actively engaging in personal and professional development and by sharing their learning experiences with their team.

Behavioral Practices:

- **Pursue ongoing education:** Regularly engage in learning activities, such as attending workshops, enrolling in courses, or reading books related to your field. Share your learning experiences with your team to inspire them to do the same.

- **Be open about your learning journey:** Talk openly about the skills you are working to develop and the knowledge you are seeking to gain. This transparency encourages your team to view learning as a shared journey.

- **Set learning goals:** Set specific learning goals for yourself and encourage your team to do the same. Regularly review these goals and assess your progress, adjusting as needed to stay on track.

By leading by example, you demonstrate the importance of continuous learning and inspire your team to prioritize their own development.

2. Creating a Learning Culture

Leaders committed to continuous learning work to create a culture where learning is encouraged, supported, and celebrated. They provide opportunities for their team to learn and grow, both individually and collectively.

Behavioral Practices:

- **Offer learning opportunities:** Provide your team with access to learning resources, such as training programs, workshops, online courses, and mentorship opportunities. Encourage them to take advantage of these resources to enhance their skills and knowledge.

- **Encourage knowledge sharing:** Foster a culture of knowledge sharing by encouraging team members to share what they've learned with others. This can be done through presentations, workshops, or informal discussions.

- **Celebrate learning achievements:** Recognize and celebrate the learning achievements of your team members. This not only reinforces the value of learning but also motivates others to pursue their own learning goals.

By creating a learning culture, you ensure that continuous learning becomes a central part of your team's identity and that everyone is committed to ongoing growth and development.

3. Encouraging Reflection and Self-Assessment

Continuous learning involves not only acquiring new knowledge but also reflecting on what you've learned and assessing your progress. Leaders committed to continuous learning encourage their team to regularly reflect on their experiences and to use self-assessment as a tool for growth.

Behavioral Practices:

- **Promote regular reflection:** Encourage your team to regularly reflect on their learning experiences, whether through journaling, discussions, or self-assessment exercises. This reflection helps them to internalize what they've learned and to identify areas for further growth.

- **Facilitate feedback:** Create an environment where feedback is valued and regularly provided. Encourage team members to seek feedback from their peers, supervisors, and mentors as a way to enhance their learning and development.

- **Use self-assessment tools:** Provide your team with self-assessment tools that help them evaluate their skills, knowledge, and progress. Encourage them to set learning goals based on their self-assessments and to regularly review and adjust these goals.

By encouraging reflection and self-assessment, you help your team to take ownership of their learning and to continuously strive for improvement.

4. Supporting Risk-Taking and Experimentation

Leaders who are committed to continuous learning understand that learning often involves taking risks and trying new things. They create an environment where experimentation is encouraged and where mistakes are viewed as opportunities for growth.

Behavioral Practices:

- **Encourage experimentation:** Support your team in trying new approaches, even if there is a risk of failure. Emphasize that experimentation is a key part of learning and that mistakes are valuable learning experiences.

- **Provide a safe environment:** Create a safe environment where team members feel comfortable taking risks and making mistakes. Ensure that they know that failure is not only acceptable but expected as part of the learning process.

- **Celebrate learning from failure:** When mistakes happen, focus on what can be learned rather than on the mistake itself. Celebrate the learning that comes from failure and encourage your team to apply these lessons moving forward.

By supporting risk-taking and experimentation, you foster a culture of continuous learning where innovation and growth are the norm.

Science-based Insight

Neuroscience research has shown that continuous learning has a profound impact on the brain's structure and function. The brain's ability to change and adapt, known as neuroplasticity, is enhanced through continuous learning, leading to the development of new neural connections and the strengthening of existing ones. This neuroplasticity supports cognitive flexibility, creativity, and problem-solving—key skills for effective leadership.

When leaders engage in continuous learning, they activate the brain's reward system, which includes the release of dopamine. Dopamine is a neurotransmitter associated with motivation, pleasure, and the reinforcement of positive behavior. The release of dopamine during learning experiences enhances focus, memory retention, and overall cognitive function, making it easier for leaders to acquire and apply new knowledge and skills (BMC Neuroscience, 2023).

Moreover, continuous learning stimulates the brain's prefrontal cortex, the area responsible for higher-order thinking, decision-making, and executive function. By regularly engaging in learning activities, leaders strengthen their cognitive abilities, improve their problem-solving skills, and enhance their capacity for strategic thinking (Bazzari & Parri, 2019).

By fostering a commitment to continuous learning, leaders can create a neurochemical environment that supports growth, innovation, and adaptability, all of which are critical for building a high-performing workplace culture.

Putting pen to paper

Exercise: The Continuous Learning Plan

Objective: To create a personalized, continuous learning plan that will help you develop your skills, expand your knowledge, and enhance your leadership effectiveness.

Instructions:

1. **Assess your current learning practices:** Begin by reflecting on your current approach to learning. Consider the following questions:

    - How often do you engage in learning activities, such as reading, attending workshops, or taking courses?

    - What are the key areas where you would like to develop your skills and knowledge?

    - How do you incorporate learning into your daily routine?

    - How do you encourage and support learning within your team?

2. **Identify learning goals:** Based on your self-assessment, identify specific learning goals that align with your personal and professional development needs. These goals should be actionable, measurable, and focused on areas where you want to grow. For example:

    - "I will read one leadership book each month to enhance my knowledge of leadership theories and practices."

    - "I will attend at least two industry conferences this year to stay updated on the latest trends and developments in my field."

- "I will take an online course in data analytics to improve my ability to make data-driven decisions."

3. **Create a learning schedule:** Develop a schedule that outlines when and how you will pursue your learning goals. This schedule should include regular time slots for reading, attending workshops, taking courses, and engaging in other learning activities. For example:

    - "I will dedicate 30 minutes each morning to reading a leadership book."

    - "I will attend a monthly webinar on topics related to my field."

    - "I will complete one module of my online course each week."

4. **Seek out learning resources:** Identify the resources you will need to achieve your learning goals. This might include books, online courses, workshops, conferences, or mentors. Make a list of these resources and ensure that you have access to them.

5. **Engage in reflective practice:** As you progress through your learning plan, take time to reflect on what you've learned and how you can apply it to your leadership role. Keep a journal or log where you can document your reflections, insights, and key takeaways.

6. **Share your learning with others:** Share what you've learned with your team, colleagues, or peers. This could be through

presentations, discussions, or informal conversations. Sharing your learning reinforces your knowledge and encourages others to engage in continuous learning.

7. **Monitor and adjust your plan:** Regularly review your learning plan to assess your progress and make any necessary adjustments. If you find that certain goals are no longer relevant or that new learning opportunities have emerged, update your plan accordingly.

By creating and following a continuous learning plan, you can ensure that you are consistently developing your skills, expanding your knowledge, and enhancing the effectiveness of your leadership. This commitment to learning not only benefits you but also inspires your team to prioritize their own growth and development.

Avoiding Leadership Pitfalls: The Dangers of Stagnation and Complacency

While continuous learning is essential for effective leadership, it's important to recognize the pitfalls that can arise when learning is not prioritized. Leaders who fail to commit to continuous learning risk creating a culture of stagnation, complacency, and resistance to change.

1. Stagnation and Lack of Innovation

Leaders who do not prioritize continuous learning may contribute to a culture of stagnation, where innovation is stifled and new ideas are not encouraged. This can lead to a lack of competitiveness and difficulty in adapting to change.

Consequences:

- **Decreased innovation:** A lack of commitment to continuous learning can stifle innovation, as employees may not be encouraged to explore new ideas or approaches.

- **Lower adaptability:** Organizations that do not prioritize continuous learning may struggle to adapt to change, as employees may lack the skills and knowledge needed to navigate new challenges.

- **Reduced competitiveness:** A culture of stagnation can lead to a loss of competitiveness, as the organization may fall behind in a rapidly changing market.

2. Complacency and Resistance to Change

Leaders who do not embrace continuous learning may inadvertently foster a culture of complacency, where employees are resistant to change and satisfied with the status quo. This can hinder growth and limit the organization's potential.

Consequences:

- **Decreased growth:** Complacency can lead to decreased growth, as employees may be less motivated to seek out new learning opportunities or to develop new skills.

- **Higher resistance to change:** A lack of commitment to continuous learning can lead to resistance to change, as employees may be less open to new ideas and approaches.

- **Lower engagement:** Complacency can lead to lower employee engagement, as employees may feel their development is not a priority and that there are limited opportunities for growth.

3. Missed Opportunities for Development

Leaders who do not prioritize continuous learning may miss opportunities for their own development and that of their team. This can limit the organization's ability to innovate, adapt, improvise and grow.

Consequences:

- **Missed skill development:** A lack of commitment to continuous learning can result in missed opportunities for skill development, limiting the potential of both leaders and employees.

- **Decreased effectiveness:** Leaders who do not prioritize their own learning may struggle to stay effective in a rapidly changing environment, as they may lack the knowledge and skills needed to lead successfully.

- **Limited organizational growth:** A lack of continuous learning can limit the organization's potential growth, as employees may not have the skills and knowledge needed to drive innovation and success.

Conclusion: Continuous Learning as the Engine of Leadership

Continuous learning is not just a leadership strategy; it's the engine that drives growth, innovation, and success. By committing to continuous learning, you not only get a chance to enhance your own leadership capabilities but also foster a culture of growth and development within your team. This commitment to learning is what enables organizations to adapt, innovate, and thrive in an ever-changing world.

In this chapter, we've explored how continuous learning influences leadership and organizational culture. We've discussed the mindset necessary to embrace lifelong learning, the behaviors that promote and support learning within your team, and the potential ripple effects that continuous learning can have on the organization as a whole. We've also examined the potential pitfalls of stagnation and complacency and the importance of maintaining a commitment to learning and growth in all aspects of leadership.

As you continue your leadership journey, remember that what you see is how you lead. By leading with a commitment to continuously learn, you not only strengthen your team but also lay the foundation for a high-performing, innovative, and resilient workplace culture.

In the chapters that follow, we will explore additional cognitive and behavioral practices that will help you refine your leadership approach and create a thriving, high-performing organizational culture. Together, we will uncover the full spectrum of leadership qualities that will empower you to lead with confidence, clarity, and a passion for learning.

Practice Nr. 9: Recognition and Appreciation

Recognition and appreciation are fundamental components of effective leadership. When leaders actively recognize and appreciate the efforts and achievements of their team members, they foster a culture of motivation, engagement, and loyalty. These practices are not just about boosting morale—they are about creating a positive and supportive environment where individuals feel valued and empowered to excel.

In this chapter of *The Mirror Effect: What You See, Is How You Lead!*, we will explore the importance of recognition and appreciation in leadership. We will examine the mindset required to genuinely value and celebrate the contributions of others and the behaviors that reinforce a culture of recognition within your team. Additionally, we will delve into the neurological and psychological impact of recognition and appreciation on employee engagement, performance, and overall workplace culture.

D. was the manager of a logistics company that operated with military precision. D. was a no-nonsense kind of leader, with a strong work ethic and a belief that everyone on his team should simply do their jobs without needing constant praise or acknowledgment. He often said, "We're just doing our jobs and getting paid for it, so why should we say thank you and well done all the time?" This mindset was rooted in his own upbringing—growing up, D. had rarely been acknowledged for his successes. His parents instilled in him the belief that doing a good job was expected, not something that warranted praise.

Under D.'s leadership, the company was running efficiently, but something was missing. The team was competent, but morale was low, and there was a noticeable lack of enthusiasm. People did their work, but there was little camaraderie or excitement. Turnover rates were higher than D. would have liked, and he couldn't understand why his team wasn't more engaged despite the company's success.

One day, after another long day of work, a senior employee named R. approached D. privately. She had been with the company for several years and had seen how the lack of recognition was affecting her colleagues. "D.," she began cautiously, "I know we're all here to do our jobs, and we're paid for it, but I think the team is really struggling with motivation. People are feeling unappreciated. They work hard, but it's like no one notices. A simple thank you, or acknowledgment could go a long way."

D. frowned, not entirely convinced. "But isn't that what they're supposed to do? They're doing their jobs, and they're compensated for it. Why should I have to thank them for something they're already expected to do?"

R. sighed, seeing how deeply ingrained this belief was in D. "I understand where you're coming from, but it's not just about the paycheck. People need to feel valued for their contributions. Recognition and appreciation aren't just about being polite— they're about motivating the team and showing them that their efforts matter."

D. was silent for a moment, pondering her words. He respected R. and knew she wasn't one to complain without reason. But the idea of regularly acknowledging his team's work felt foreign to him. He decided to seek my advice, knowing that something needed to change but unsure of how to go about it.

During our conversation, I asked him, "D., why do you think recognition and appreciation are important, even if people are just doing their jobs?"

He hesitated, then admitted, "I didn't grow up with a lot of praise. I was taught that doing your job well was expected, not something to be celebrated. But now I'm wondering if that's why the team seems so disengaged. Maybe they need more than just a paycheck."

"Exactly," I replied. "Recognition and appreciation are powerful motivators. When people feel valued, they're more likely to go above and beyond, to be engaged and invested in their work. It's not just about saying thank you—it's about building a positive and supportive work environment where people feel their contributions are noticed and appreciated. How do you think your team would respond if you started acknowledging their efforts more?"

D. looked thoughtful. "I suppose it could make a difference. I've always assumed that because I don't need that kind of recognition, they wouldn't either. But maybe I've been wrong."

"Everyone is different," I said. "While some people might not need constant praise, others do. And even those who don't expect it can still benefit from feeling appreciated. Why not try it and see how your team responds?"

Determined to make a change, D. decided to take R.'s advice to heart. The next day, he called a meeting with his team. Instead of diving straight into the day's tasks as he usually did, he took a moment to acknowledge the team's hard work. "I want to start by saying thank you," he began, feeling slightly awkward but sincere. "I know I haven't said this enough, but I appreciate the effort each of you puts in every day. Rachel, your work on the last project was outstanding, and it didn't go unnoticed. Tom, the way you handled that difficult client was impressive. I want you all to know that I see the hard work you're doing, and it makes a difference."

The team was visibly surprised by D.'s words. They weren't used to hearing praise from him, but they appreciated it. Over the next few weeks, D. made a conscious effort to recognize his team's efforts more regularly. He started sending out thank-you emails, acknowledging both small and large contributions, and he encouraged his managers to do the same.

To D.'s surprise, he began to notice a change in the team's dynamics. People seemed more motivated and more willing to take on challenges, and there was a renewed sense of camaraderie in the office. Team members started to share their ideas more freely, knowing that their contributions would be valued. The atmosphere became more positive, and the turnover rate began to decrease.

Reflecting on the experience, D. realized that recognition and appreciation weren't just about being nice—they were essential for building a motivated and engaged team. By acknowledging his team's efforts, he was able to create a work environment where people felt valued and driven to excel. D. learned that leadership isn't just about getting the job done; it's about inspiring others to do their best by showing them that their work matters. Recognition and appreciation became integral to his leadership style, and as a result, his team thrived.

Understanding Recognition and Appreciation in Leadership

Recognition in leadership involves acknowledging the efforts, contributions, and achievements of team members. It's about making sure that people know their work is noticed and valued. Appreciation goes a step further—it's about expressing gratitude for the unique qualities and efforts of individuals beyond just their achievements. Together, recognition and appreciation create a powerful combination that drives motivation, fosters engagement, and builds a strong sense of community within the organization.

Leaders who prioritize recognition and appreciation understand that these practices are not just about giving praise—they are about cultivating an environment where everyone feels seen, valued, and motivated to contribute their best. This creates a positive feedback loop where employees are more engaged, more productive, and more likely to stay with the organization in the long run.

The Mindset of a Leader Who Values Recognition and Appreciation

To lead with recognition and appreciation, you must first adopt a mindset that genuinely values the contributions of others and understands the impact that recognition and gratitude can have on motivation and engagement. This mindset involves being attentive, generous with praise, and sincere in your expressions of gratitude.

1. Valuing the Contributions of Others

Leaders who excel in recognition and appreciation genuinely value the contributions of their team members. They understand that every individual plays a vital role in the success of an organization and that acknowledging these contributions is essential for fostering consistency, motivation, and engagement.

Mindset: Embrace the belief that every contribution, no matter how small, is valuable. Recognize that by acknowledging the efforts of others, you build a culture of respect, motivation, and collective success.

2. Being Generous with Praise

Effective leaders are generous with praise—they don't wait for grand achievements to recognize their team members. Instead, they consistently acknowledge progress, effort, and improvement, understanding that regular recognition is key to maintaining high levels of engagement.

Mindset: Develop a habit of noticing and celebrating the efforts and progress of your team. Understand that frequent and meaningful recognition is a powerful motivator and a cornerstone of a positive workplace culture.

3. Expressing Sincere Gratitude

Appreciation is most impactful when it is sincere. Leaders who value appreciation express their gratitude in a way that is authentic and heartfelt. They understand that when people feel genuinely appreciated, they are more likely to be motivated, engaged, and committed to their work.

Mindset: Cultivate an attitude of gratitude. Make it a priority to express sincere appreciation for the efforts and contributions of your team members, recognizing the positive impact this has on their motivation and well-being.

4. Encouraging a Culture of Recognition

Leaders committed to recognition and appreciation encourage these practices throughout the organization. They understand that recognition should not only come from the top but should be a shared responsibility among all team members.

Mindset: Believe in the importance of creating a culture of recognition where everyone feels empowered to acknowledge and celebrate the contributions of others. Encourage your team to regularly express appreciation and recognition among themselves.

Behavioral Practices for Leading with Recognition and Appreciation

Once you have cultivated a mindset that values recognition and appreciation, the next step is to translate that mindset into behaviors that reinforce these practices within your team. These behaviors are crucial for creating a culture where recognition and appreciation are regularly practiced and genuinely felt.

1. Regularly Acknowledge Achievements and Efforts

Leaders who value recognition make it a point to regularly acknowledge the achievements and efforts of their team members. They understand that recognition should be timely, specific, and meaningful.

Behavioral Practices:

- **Be timely:** Recognize achievements and efforts as soon as possible after they occur. Timely recognition reinforces the connection between the effort and the reward, making it more impactful.

- **Be specific:** When giving recognition, be specific about what you are acknowledging. Instead of a generic "good job," highlight the particular action, behavior, or outcome that you are recognizing.

- **Celebrate progress:** Recognize not only the final outcomes but also the progress along the way. Celebrate milestones, small wins, and the consistent efforts that contribute to larger successes.

By regularly acknowledging achievements and efforts, you reinforce the importance of each individual's contributions and create a culture where people feel motivated to continue striving for excellence.

2. Express Gratitude in Meaningful Ways

Appreciation is most effective when it is expressed in ways that are meaningful to the recipient. Leaders who value appreciation take the time to understand how their team members prefer to be appreciated and tailor their expressions of gratitude accordingly.

Behavioral Practices:

- **Personalize your appreciation:** Consider the preferences of each team member when expressing gratitude. Some may appreciate public recognition, while others may prefer a private thank-you note or a one-on-one conversation.

- **Use a variety of methods:** Mix up your methods of expressing appreciation to keep it fresh and impactful. This includes verbal praise, written notes, recognition in team meetings, or small tokens of appreciation.

- **Be sincere:** Ensure that your expressions of gratitude are genuine and heartfelt. People can sense when appreciation is insincere, so take the time to reflect on why you are grateful and express it authentically.

By expressing gratitude in meaningful ways, you demonstrate that you value and respect each individual's unique contributions, fostering a culture of appreciation and mutual respect.

3. Encourage Peer Recognition

Leaders committed to recognition understand that it should not only come from the top but should be encouraged among peers as well. They create an environment where team members feel comfortable and empowered to recognize and appreciate each other's contributions.

Behavioral Practices:

- **Promote peer recognition:** Encourage team members to recognize each other's efforts and achievements. This can be done through formal programs, such as "Employee of the Month," or informal practices, like shout-outs in meetings.

- **Facilitate opportunities for recognition:** Create opportunities for peer recognition by setting aside time in meetings for team members to share their appreciation for one another's work. This reinforces a culture of mutual respect and collaboration.

- **Recognize peer recognition:** Acknowledge and celebrate instances of peer recognition. When team members recognize each other, highlight these moments to show that you value and support a culture of collective appreciation.

By encouraging peer recognition, you foster a sense of community and collaboration within your team, where everyone feels valued and appreciated by their colleagues.

4. Make Recognition and Appreciation a Habit

Recognition and appreciation should not be occasional or reserved for special occasions—they should be integrated into the daily fabric of your leadership and team culture. Leaders who value these practices make them a regular habit, ensuring that all team members consistently feel recognition and appreciation.

Behavioral Practices:

- **Integrate into daily routines:** Make recognition and appreciation a regular part of your daily routine. This could include starting meetings with positive feedback, sending daily or weekly thank-you notes, or setting reminders to acknowledge team members' continuous efforts.

- **Create formal recognition programs:** Implement formal recognition programs that provide structure and consistency to your recognition efforts. This could include annual awards, recognition ceremonies, or regular team celebrations.

- **Monitor and adapt:** Regularly assess the effectiveness of your recognition and appreciation efforts. Seek feedback from your team on how these practices are impacting them and make adjustments as needed to ensure they remain meaningful and impactful.

By making recognition and appreciation a habit, you create a culture where these practices are consistently reinforced, leading to higher levels of motivation, engagement, and job satisfaction.

Science-based Insight

Recognition activates the brain's reward systems, particularly dopamine and oxytocin, enhancing motivation, trust, and social bonding while also contributing to employee retention and overall performance.

A recent survey conducted by Top Workplaces (2024) highlights that organizations with strong recognition programs observed higher levels of engagement, with 83% of employees reporting that colleagues also appreciated their efforts, leading to better collaboration and motivation.

Another survey found that employees who receive consistent recognition are five times more likely to remain at their current organization. Additionally, 69% of workers said they would work harder if their efforts were better recognized, emphasizing the correlation between recognition and productivity (Vega-HR, 2023).

By fostering a culture of recognition and appreciation, leaders can create a neurochemical environment that supports motivation, engagement, and strong social bonds, all of which are critical for building a high-performing workplace culture.

Putting pen to paper

Exercise: The Recognition and Appreciation Plan

Objective: To develop a structured plan for integrating recognition and appreciation into your leadership approach and to create a culture where these practices are consistently reinforced.

Instructions:

1. **Assess your current recognition practices:** Begin by reflecting on how you currently recognize and appreciate your team members. Consider the following questions:

- How often do you recognize the efforts and achievements of your team members?

- What methods do you use to express recognition and appreciation?

- How do your team members prefer to be recognized and appreciated?

- How do you encourage peer recognition within your team?

2. **Identify areas for improvement:** Based on your self-assessment, identify specific areas where you can improve your recognition and appreciation practices. This might include increasing the frequency of recognition, using more personalized methods, or encouraging more peer recognition.

3. **Set specific goals:** Set two or three specific goals that will help you enhance your recognition and appreciation efforts. These goals should be actionable, measurable, and aligned with the areas of improvement you've identified. For example:

   - "I will recognize at least one team member's contribution and efforts each week during our team meetings."

   - "I will send personalized thank-you notes to team members after they complete major projects or reach significant milestones."

- "I will implement a peer recognition program that allows team members to nominate each other for recognition on a monthly basis."

4. **Personalize your recognition and appreciation efforts:** Consider the preferences of each team member when expressing recognition and appreciation. Take the time to understand how they like to be recognized and tailor your approach accordingly.

5. **Encourage peer recognition:** Promote a culture of peer recognition by encouraging team members to acknowledge each other's contributions. This could include setting up a formal peer recognition program or simply encouraging informal recognition in team meetings.

6. **Monitor and adjust your plan:** Regularly review your recognition and appreciation plan to assess its effectiveness. Seek feedback from your team on how these practices are impacting them and make adjustments as needed to ensure they remain meaningful and impactful.

By creating and following a recognition and appreciation plan, you can ensure that these practices are consistently reinforced, leading to higher levels of motivation, engagement, and job satisfaction within your team. This commitment to recognizing and appreciating your team members not only benefits them but also strengthens your leadership and contributes to a positive and high-performing workplace culture.

Avoiding Leadership Pitfalls: The Dangers of Neglecting Recognition and Appreciation

While recognition and appreciation are essential for effective leadership, it's important to recognize the pitfalls that can arise when these practices are neglected. Leaders who fail to acknowledge the contributions of their team members risk creating a culture of disengagement, low morale, and high turnover.

1. Disengagement and Low Morale

Leaders who neglect recognition and appreciation may contribute to a culture of disengagement and low morale. When employees feel that their efforts go unnoticed or unappreciated, they are less likely to be motivated and engaged in their work.

Consequences:

- **Decreased motivation:** A lack of recognition and appreciation can lead to decreased motivation, as employees may feel that their hard work is not being valued or rewarded.

- **Lower engagement:** When employees do not feel appreciated, they are less likely to be engaged in their work, leading to lower productivity and job satisfaction.

- **Higher turnover:** Disengaged employees are more likely to leave the organization in search of a workplace that will value and appreciate them.

2. Reduced Performance and Productivity

Leaders who fail to recognize and appreciate their team members may see a decline in performance and productivity. Without the motivation and encouragement that recognition provides, employees may struggle to maintain high levels of performance.

Consequences:

- **Lower productivity:** A lack of recognition and appreciation can lead to lower productivity, as employees may not feel motivated to give their best effort.

- **Decreased quality of work:** When employees do not feel appreciated, they may be less likely to take pride in their work, leading to a decline in the quality of their output.

- **Missed opportunities:** Neglecting recognition and appreciation can result in missed opportunities to celebrate progress, reinforce positive behaviors, and motivate employees to achieve their goals.

3. Erosion of Trust and Loyalty

Leaders who do not prioritize recognition and appreciation may erode trust and loyalty within their team. Employees who feel unappreciated usually become disengaged, distrustful, and less committed to the organization.

Consequences:

- **Loss of trust:** A lack of recognition and appreciation can erode trust between leaders and employees, leading to a breakdown in communication and collaboration.

- **Decreased loyalty:** Employees who do not feel valued are less likely to be loyal to the organization, increasing the risk of turnover and loss of talent.

- **Negative workplace culture:** Neglecting recognition and appreciation can contribute to a negative workplace culture, where employees feel unappreciated, demotivated, and disconnected from the organization's mission.

Conclusion: Recognition and Appreciation as Pillars of Leadership

Recognition and appreciation are not just leadership strategies; they are the pillars that support motivation, engagement, and a positive workplace culture. By leading with recognition, you acknowledge the efforts and achievements of your team, reinforcing the value of their contributions. By leading with appreciation, you express gratitude for the unique qualities and efforts of each individual, fostering a sense of belonging and commitment.

In this chapter, we've explored how recognition and appreciation influence leadership and organizational culture. We've discussed the mindset necessary to genuinely value and celebrate the contributions of others, the behaviors that reinforce a culture of recognition within your team, and the ripple effects that recognition and appreciation have on the organization as a whole. We've also examined the potential pitfalls of neglecting these practices and the importance of consistently recognizing and appreciating your team's efforts.

As you continue your leadership journey, remember that what you see is how you lead. By leading with recognition and appreciation, you not only strengthen your team but also lay the foundation for a high-performing, motivated, and engaged workplace culture.

In the chapters that follow, we will explore additional cognitive and behavioral practices that will help you refine your leadership approach and create a thriving, high-performing organizational culture. Together, we will uncover the full spectrum of leadership qualities that will empower you to lead with confidence, clarity, and a genuine appreciation for the contributions of others.

Practice Nr. 10:
Collaboration and Team Orientation

Collaboration and team orientation are vital elements of effective leadership. Leaders who foster a collaborative environment and prioritize team orientation understand that the success of the organization depends not on individual achievements but on the collective efforts of the entire team. By cultivating a culture of collaboration, leaders empower their teams to work together, share knowledge, and achieve goals that would be impossible to reach alone.

In this chapter of *The Mirror Effect: What You See, Is How You Lead!*, we will explore the importance of collaboration and team orientation in leadership. We will examine the mindset required to prioritize collective success and the behaviors that reinforce a collaborative culture within your team. Additionally, we will delve into the neurological and psychological impact of collaboration and team orientation on employee engagement, performance, and overall organizational success.

I once worked with K., a team leader of a tech company. K. was highly intelligent and driven and had an impressive track record of leading successful projects. She was known for her ability to solve complex problems and make quick decisions, often preferring to work independently to ensure things were done to her exact standards. K. believed that relying too much on others could slow down progress, so she often took on the bulk of the work herself, viewing collaboration as more of a formality than a necessity.

Her team, composed of talented engineers and designers, was often left out of the decision-making process. K. would assign tasks and expect her team members to execute them without much discussion or input. She felt that she was protecting them from the burden of responsibility and believed that by handling the key decisions herself, she was sparing them the stress. However, her approach led to an unintended consequence: her team felt disconnected, undervalued, and increasingly disengaged.

As the company began to scale rapidly, the demands on the product development team intensified. K. found herself overwhelmed, struggling to keep up with the workload and increasingly frustrated that her team wasn't stepping up as she expected them to. Deadlines started slipping, and her quality of work began to suffer. The team's morale was at an all-time low, and tensions were soon rising.

During one particularly challenging project, the team was tasked with developing a new product feature that was crucial to the company's upcoming launch. K., as usual, took on the planning and decision-making herself, assigning specific tasks to each team member without much explanation or input. As the deadline approached, it became clear that the project was in trouble—communication breakdowns were rampant, and the lack of collaboration led to numerous errors and inefficiencies.

Feeling the pressure, K. reached out to me for advice. During our conversation, I asked her, "K., how do you view collaboration and team input in your projects?"

She hesitated before replying, "I know collaboration is important, but honestly, I've always felt that it's faster and more efficient if I handle the critical decisions myself. I just want to make sure everything is done right."

"But what's been the result of that approach?" I asked gently.

K. sighed, clearly frustrated. "The team isn't performing the way I need them to. They're not taking ownership, and it feels like everything is falling on my shoulders. I don't understand why they're not stepping up."

"K.," I said, "collaboration isn't just about dividing tasks; it's about building a sense of ownership and shared responsibility. When your team feels involved in the decision-making process and knows that their ideas are valued, they're more likely to take ownership and contribute their best work. How might things change if you started involving your team more in the planning and decision-making?"

K. looked thoughtful. "I've always been afraid that too much collaboration would slow us down, but maybe I've been going about it the wrong way. I'm willing to try something different if it means getting the team more engaged."

Determined to make a change, K. called a meeting with her team. This time, instead of dictating the plan, she opened up the floor for discussion. "I realize that I've been taking on too much myself," she admitted. "I want to involve all of you more in the planning and decision-making process. I know each of you has valuable insights and ideas, and I want us to work together to make this project a success."

The team was initially surprised by K.'s shift in approach, but they quickly responded to the opportunity to contribute. As they began to share their ideas and perspectives, the atmosphere in the room changed. K. listened carefully, encouraged discussion, and even acknowledged that some of the ideas were better than her initial plans. The team collaborated to refine the project plan, with each member taking ownership of specific aspects based on their strengths and expertise.

Over the next few weeks, the team worked more cohesively than ever before. With a clear sense of ownership and a shared goal, they communicated more effectively, supported each other, and solved problems collaboratively. The project, which had once seemed doomed to fail, came together smoothly and was completed ahead of schedule. The new feature was well-received by customers, and the company's launch was a success.

Reflecting on the experience, K. realized that collaboration and team orientation were not just about getting the job done—they were about fostering a sense of collective ownership and harnessing the diverse talents within her team. By trusting her team and involving them in the decision-making process, she was able to create a more engaged, motivated, and high-performing team. K. learned that true leadership involves not just guiding the team but empowering them to contribute their best, ensuring that everyone is working together toward a common goal. From that point on, collaboration became a core value in her leadership approach, and her team thrived as a result.

Understanding Collaboration and Team Orientation in Leadership

Collaboration in leadership involves creating an environment where team members can work together effectively, sharing ideas, resources, and responsibilities to achieve common goals. Team orientation goes hand in hand with collaboration—it's about aligning the efforts of individuals with the broader objectives of the team and the organization. Leaders who prioritize collaboration and team orientation recognize that the strength of the team lies in its ability to function as a cohesive unit, where each member contributes their unique strengths to achieve shared success while covering each other's weaknesses.

A culture of collaboration and team orientation not only enhances productivity but also fosters a sense of belonging and mutual respect among team members. When leaders actively promote these values, they create an organization where innovation flourishes, challenges are overcome collectively, and every member feels valued and motivated to contribute their best.

The Mindset of a Leader Who Values Collaboration and Team Orientation

To lead with collaboration and team orientation, you must first adopt a mindset that values collective success over individual achievement. This mindset involves recognizing the power of teamwork, embracing diverse perspectives, and fostering an environment where everyone feels empowered to contribute.

1. Valuing Collective Success Over Individual Achievement

Leaders who prioritize collaboration and team orientation understand that the success of the organization depends on the collective efforts of the entire team. They recognize that individual achievements are significant but that true success is achieved when everyone works together toward a common goal.

Mindset: Embrace the belief that collective success is more powerful than individual achievement. Recognize that by working together, the team can achieve far more than any one person could alone.

199

2. Embracing Diverse Perspectives

Effective collaboration requires leaders to embrace and value diverse perspectives. Leaders who prioritize team orientation understand that each team member brings unique skills, experiences, and viewpoints that contribute to the team's overall success.

Mindset: Develop an appreciation for the diverse perspectives within your team. Understand that by embracing diversity, you enhance the team's ability to innovate, solve problems, and achieve shared goals.

3. Fostering a Sense of Belonging and Inclusion

Leaders committed to collaboration and team orientation create an environment where everyone feels included, respected, and valued. They understand that a sense of belonging is essential for effective teamwork and that when team members feel connected to one another, they are more likely to collaborate effectively as well as efficiently.

Mindset: Cultivate a mindset that prioritizes inclusion and belonging. Recognize that when team members feel valued and included, they are more motivated to contribute their best to the team's success.

4. Encouraging Open Communication and Shared Accountability

Collaboration thrives in an environment where open communication is encouraged and accountability is shared. Leaders who value team orientation ensure that everyone has a voice and that responsibilities are distributed equitably across the team.

Mindset: Believe in the importance of open communication and shared accountability. Understand that by fostering an environment where everyone can contribute and share responsibility, you create a stronger, more cohesive team.

Behavioral Practices for Leading with Collaboration and Team Orientation

Once you have cultivated a mindset that values collaboration and team orientation, the next step is to translate that mindset into behaviors that reinforce these principles within your team. These behaviors are crucial for creating a culture where collaboration is the norm and where the team's success is prioritized over individual accomplishments.

1. Promoting Open Communication and Information Sharing

Leaders who value collaboration understand that open communication is the foundation of effective teamwork. They encourage their team members to share information, ideas, and feedback freely, creating an environment where collaboration and work can thrive.

Behavioral Practices:

- **Facilitate regular team meetings:** Hold regular team meetings where everyone has the opportunity to share updates, ideas, and concerns. Ensure that these meetings are structured to encourage participation and open dialogue.

- **Encourage cross-functional communication:** Promote communication across different departments and functions within the organization. This helps to break down silos and encourages collaboration between teams with diverse expertise.

- **Use collaborative tools:** Implement collaborative tools and platforms that facilitate information sharing and communication. Encourage your team to use these tools to stay connected and to collaborate more effectively.

By promoting open communication and information sharing, you create a culture where collaboration is seamless and everyone is aligned with the team's goals.

2. Encouraging Collaborative Problem-Solving

Leaders who prioritize collaboration and team orientation encourage their teams to solve problems together. They understand that collaborative problem-solving leads to more innovative solutions and that it strengthens the bonds between team members.

Behavioral Practices:

- **Facilitate brainstorming sessions:** When faced with challenges, bring your team together for brainstorming sessions. Encourage everyone to contribute their ideas and perspectives and work together to identify the best solutions.

- **Involve the team in decision-making:** Whenever possible, involve your team in the decision-making process. This not only leads to better decisions but also ensures that everyone feels invested in the outcomes.

- **Promote a collaborative mindset:** Encourage your team to approach problems with a collaborative mindset, where everyone's input is valued and where the focus is on finding solutions together.

By encouraging collaborative problem-solving, you strengthen the team's ability to work together effectively and overcome challenges as a cohesive unit.

3. Recognizing and Celebrating Team Achievements

Leaders committed to team orientation recognize and celebrate the achievements of the entire team rather than focusing solely on individual accomplishments. They understand that celebrating team success reinforces the importance of collaboration and motivates the team to continue working together.

Behavioral Practices:

- **Celebrate team milestones:** Recognize and celebrate important team milestones, such as the completion of a major project or the achievement of a shared goal. This reinforces the value of teamwork and collective success.

- **Acknowledge individual contributions to team success:** While celebrating team achievements, also take the time to acknowledge the individual contributions that made those achievements possible. This ensures that everyone feels valued for their role in the team's success.

- **Hold team-building events:** Organize team-building events and activities that strengthen relationships within the team and celebrate the team's collective efforts.

By recognizing and celebrating team achievements, you reinforce the importance of collaboration and create a culture where collective success is valued and celebrated.

4. Building Trust and Mutual Respect

Collaboration and team orientation thrive in an environment of trust and mutual respect. Leaders who value these principles work to build and maintain trust within their teams, ensuring that everyone feels respected and valued.

Behavioral Practices.

- **Foster trust through transparency:** Be transparent in your communication and decision-making processes. When team members understand the reasoning behind decisions, they are more likely to trust the process and each other.

- **Encourage mutual respect:** Promote a culture of mutual respect within your team, where everyone's ideas and contributions are valued. Address any issues of disrespect or conflict promptly to maintain a positive team dynamic.

- **Lead by example:** Demonstrate trust and respect in your interactions with team members. By modeling these behaviors, you set the standard for how team members should treat each other.

By building trust and mutual respect, you create a strong foundation for collaboration and team orientation, where everyone feels supported and valued.

Science-based Insight

Recent studies demonstrate how team synchronization enhances collaboration and strengthens social bonds. Research from Wharton Executive Education (2024) highlights that effective teamwork is deeply tied to neural synchrony, where the brain activity of team members aligns during successful collaboration. This synchrony is reinforced by neurotransmitters like oxytocin, known for fostering trust and bonding within teams, and dopamine, which rewards team members with a sense of pleasure and motivation when they achieve shared goals.

These findings support the importance of creating a collaborative environment where both neurochemical and cognitive processes are optimized and enhance team cohesion, creativity, and performance.

Putting pen to paper

Exercise: The Team Collaboration Plan

Objective: To develop a structured plan for fostering collaboration and team orientation within your leadership approach and to create a culture where these practices are consistently reinforced.

Instructions:

1. **Assess your current collaboration practices:** Begin by reflecting on how your team currently collaborates. Consider the following questions:

   - How often do team members work together on projects or tasks?

   - What methods and tools do you use to facilitate collaboration?

   - How do you encourage open communication and information sharing within your team?

   - How do you recognize and celebrate team achievements?

2. **Identify areas for improvement:** Based on your self-assessment, identify specific areas where you can enhance your collaboration and team orientation practices. This might include increasing opportunities for cross-functional collaboration, improving communication tools, or implementing new methods for recognizing team achievements.

3. **Set specific goals:** Set two or three specific goals that will help you strengthen collaboration and team orientation within your team. These goals should be actionable, measurable, and aligned with the areas for improvement you've identified. For example:

   - "I will increase opportunities for cross-functional collaboration by organizing quarterly interdepartmental projects."

   - "I will implement a new collaborative platform to improve communication and information sharing within the team."

   - "I will recognize and celebrate team achievements by holding monthly team-building events and acknowledging collective successes in team meetings."

4. **Develop a collaboration schedule:** Create a schedule that outlines when and how you will promote collaboration and team orientation within your team. This schedule should

include regular time slots for collaborative activities, team meetings, and recognition of team achievements. For example:

- "I will hold weekly team meetings where we discuss ongoing projects and identify opportunities for collaboration."

- "I will set aside one day each month for team-building activities that strengthen relationships and encourage collaboration."

- "I will organize quarterly cross-functional projects that bring together team members from different departments to work on shared goals."

5. **Foster a collaborative mindset:** Encourage your team to adopt a collaborative mindset by promoting open communication, shared accountability, and mutual respect. Create opportunities for team members to work together and support each other in achieving common goals.

6. **Monitor and adjust your plan:** Regularly review your collaboration and team orientation plan to assess its effectiveness. Seek feedback from your team on how these practices are impacting them and make adjustments accordingly to ensure they remain meaningful and impactful.

By creating and following a team collaboration plan, you can ensure that collaboration and team orientation are consistently reinforced, leading to higher levels of innovation, engagement, and collective success within your team. This commitment to teamwork and shared goals not only benefits your team but also strengthens your leadership and contributes to a positive and high-performing workplace culture.

Avoiding Leadership Pitfalls: The Dangers of Silos and Individualism

While collaboration and team orientation are essential for effective leadership, it's important to recognize the pitfalls that can arise when these principles are neglected. Leaders who fail to prioritize collaboration or who encourage individualism may create a culture of silos, competition, and disengagement.

1. Silos and Lack of Communication

Leaders who do not prioritize collaboration may inadvertently create a culture of silos, where teams or departments work in isolation from one another. This can lead to lack of communication, duplication of efforts, and missed opportunities for collaboration.

Consequences:

- **Decreased innovation:** Silos limit the exchange of ideas and information, reducing opportunities for innovation and creativity.

- **Lower productivity:** When teams work in silos, they may duplicate efforts or miss out on synergies that could potentially enhance productivity.

- **Reduced organizational alignment:** Silos can lead to misalignment between teams or departments, making it harder to achieve organizational goals.

2. Individualism and Competition

Leaders who emphasize individual achievement over team success may foster a culture of individualism and competition. This can lead to lack of collaboration, as team members focus on their own goals rather than the success of the team.

Consequences:

- **Decreased teamwork:** A focus on individual achievement can undermine teamwork, as team members may prioritize their own success over the success of the group.

- **Higher conflict:** Individualism and competition can lead to conflict within the team, as team members compete for recognition or resources.

- **Lower morale:** A culture of individualism can lead to lower morale, as team members may feel isolated or unsupported in their efforts.

3. Disengagement and Turnover

Leaders who do not foster a collaborative environment may see higher levels of disengagement and turnover. When team members do not feel connected to their team or the organization's goals, they are more likely to become disengaged and seek opportunities elsewhere.

Consequences:

- **Lower engagement:** A lack of collaboration can lead to disengagement, as team members may feel disconnected from their work and from the organization's mission.

- **Higher turnover:** Disengaged employees are more likely to leave the organization, leading to higher turnover and loss of valuable talent.

- **Reduced organizational success:** Disengagement and turnover can undermine the organization's ability to achieve its goals, as it loses the collective strength of its teams.

Conclusion: Collaboration and Team Orientation as Pillars of Leadership

Collaboration and team orientation are not just leadership strategies; they are the pillars that support collective success, innovation, and organizational alignment. By leading with collaboration, you bring people together, harnessing their diverse strengths to achieve shared goals. By leading with team orientation, you ensure that everyone is working toward the same vision, creating a cohesive and motivated workforce.

In this chapter, we've explored how collaboration and team orientation influence leadership and organizational culture. We've discussed the mindset necessary to prioritize collective success, the behaviors that reinforce a collaborative culture within your team, and the ripple effects that collaboration and team orientation have on the organization as a whole. We've also examined the potential pitfalls of silos and individualism and the importance of maintaining a commitment to teamwork and shared goals in all aspects of leadership.

EPILOGUE

Reflecting on the Journey

As we reach the conclusion of *The Mirror Effect: What You See, Is How You Lead!*, it's time to reflect on the journey we've taken together. Leadership is a journey, not a destination. It's a continuous process of self-discovery, growth, and adaptation. The principles we've explored in this book—empathy and emotional intelligence, visionary thinking, transparency, resilience, empowerment, and more—are not just traits to be learned and mastered; they are ongoing practices that require reflection, commitment, and action.

Looking Back: The Power of Reflection

Throughout this book, we've seen how the behaviors and mindsets of leaders can shape organizational culture, influence team dynamics, and drive success. We've shared stories of leaders who faced challenges, made mistakes, and ultimately grew into more effective and compassionate leaders. These stories are a reminder that leadership is a deeply personal journey. It's about recognizing your strengths, acknowledging your weaknesses, and being willing to learn and evolve.

The mirror effect teaches us that what we see in ourselves—our values, beliefs, and behaviors—is reflected in how we lead others. As you've explored these chapters, I hope you've taken the time to reflect on your own leadership style, to consider how your actions and mindset influence those around you, and to identify areas where you can grow and improve.

Looking Forward: The Journey Continues

As you continue your leadership journey, remember that growth doesn't happen overnight. It's a gradual process that requires patience, persistence, and a commitment to continuous learning. The lessons and strategies we've discussed in this book are tools to help you navigate the challenges of leadership, but they are only the beginning.

Leadership is dynamic, and so are the environments in which we lead. The world is constantly changing, and as a leader, you must be prepared to adapt, innovate, and lead with integrity, empathy, and vision. By embracing the principles of the mirror effect, you can create a positive and lasting impact on your team, your organization, and beyond.

A Final Reflection: What Do You See?

As we close this book, I invite you to take one final moment to look in the mirror—both literally and metaphorically. What do you see? How have you grown as a leader throughout this journey? What changes will you make moving forward to ensure that you are leading in a way that reflects your true values and intentions?

Remember, leadership is not about being perfect; it's about being authentic. It's about leading with purpose, integrity, and a genuine commitment to the well-being and success of others. When you lead with these qualities, you create a ripple effect that touches everyone around you, inspiring them to grow, to contribute, and to succeed.

The Legacy of Leadership

Ultimately, the legacy you leave as a leader will be defined not by your titles or achievements but by the positive impact you've had on others. By leading with empathy, vision, transparency, resilience, empowerment, and trust, you can create a legacy that inspires, uplifts, and empowers others to reach their full potential.

As you move forward, I encourage you to continue reflecting, learning, and growing as a leader. Use the tools and insights you've gained from this book to build a thriving, high-performing organizational culture where everyone feels valued, motivated, and empowered to contribute their best.

Thank you for embarking on this journey with me. I am confident that as you continue to grow as a leader, you will make a profound and positive impact on the lives of those you lead. Remember, what you see is how you lead—so always strive to see the best in yourself and in those around you.

Your Leadership Journey

This is not the end of your leadership journey—it's just the beginning. As you close this book, I challenge you to take the lessons you've learned and put them into action. Reflect on what you've discovered about yourself, set new goals for your growth, and lead with the intention to make a difference. The mirror effect is a powerful tool—use it to create the legacy of leadership you aspire to leave behind.

Here's to your continued growth, your unwavering commitment to leadership, and the positive impact you will make on the world.

With gratitude and encouragement,

Valentina Kordi

References:

Goleman, D. (1995). Emotional Intelligence. New York: Bantam Books, 1995. Print

Salovey, P., & Mayer, J. D. (1990). Emotional Intelligence. Imagination, Cognition and Personality, 9(3), 185-211.

Henley, D. (2019). Understanding Mirror Neurons to Become a More Emotionally Intelligent Leader. Training Industry. Retrieved from: https://trainingindustry.com/articles/leadership/understanding-mirror-neurons-to-become-a-more-emotionally-intelligent-leader/

Orloff, J. (2022). How the Brain's Mirror Neurons Affect Empathy. Psychology Today. Retrieved from:

https://www.psychologytoday.com/us/blog/emotional-freedom/202206/how-the-brains-mirror-neurons-affect-empathy

Dame Leadership. (2024). Decoding the brain science of effective delegation. Retrieved from https://www.dameleadership.com

Baumgartner, T., Heinrichs, M., Vonlanthen, A., Fischbacher, U., & Fehr, E. (2008). Oxytocin shapes the neural circuitry of trust and trust adaptation in humans. Neuron, 58(4), 639–650.

Ross, S. (2024). The Neurobiology of Trust and its Impact on Team Performance. SanaRoss.com.

Bartz, J. A., Zaki, J., Bolger, N., & Ochsner, K. N. (2011). Social effects of oxytocin in humans: context and person matter. Trends in Cognitive Science, 15(7), 301-309.

Frontiers in Psychology. (2020). The reciprocal relationship between openness and creativity: from neurobiology to multicultural environments. Retrieved from https://www.frontiersin.org

Brocardo, P. S., et al. (2023). Exploring the role of neuroplasticity in development, aging, and neurodegeneration. Brain Sciences, 13(12), 1610.

Lorsch, Z. S., et al. (2019). Stress resilience is promoted by a Zfp189-driven transcriptional network in the prefrontal cortex. Nature Neuroscience, 22(9), 1413-1423.

Kennedy, J. J. (2021). Neuro-Resilience: The brain's ability to recover from stress. Psychology Today.

Stanford. (2017). How 'Love Hormone' Oxytocin Spurs Sociability. Neuroscience News. Retrieved from https://neurosciencenews.com/oxytocin-sociability-7623/

Kennedy, J. J. (2021). Neurotransmitters of Leadership. Psychology Today.

Zak, P. J. (2017). The Neuroscience of Trust. Harvard Business Review.

Bazzari, A. H., & Parri, H. R. (2019). Neuromodulators and Long-Term Synaptic Plasticity in Learning and Memory. Brain Sciences, 9(11), 300.

BMC Neuroscience. (2023). Developmental changes in human dopamine neurotransmission: cortical receptors and terminators. BMC Neuroscience.

Top Workplaces. (2024). Employee Recognition: Improve Your Workplace Culture in 2024. Top Workplaces Research Lab. Retrieved from https://www.topworkplaces.com

Vega-HR. (2023). The Impact of Employee Recognition on Retention and Engagement. Vega-HR. Retrieved from https://www.vega-hr.com